CARYS D. COBURN

Carys D. Coburn's *BÁN* was shortlisted for the Susan Smith Blackburn Award, and subsequently produced by the Abbey Theatre. They were the winner of the Verity Bargate Award 2017 for *Citysong* – co-produced by Soho Theatre, the Abbey Theatre, and Galway International Arts Festival. Other plays include *Absent The Wrong* (Best Production at Dublin Fringe 2022) and *HOTHOUSE* (Best Production at Dublin Fringe 2023). One of the founders of MALAPROP, their work together won acclaim for its distinctive blend of nerdiness and tenderness.

Short work includes *Me, Sara* for the Abbey's Priming the Canon, *ALASIALIAS* for Paines Plough's *Come To Where I'm From*, and *Our Mother, My Daughters* for Draíocht Blanchardstown's HOME Theatre. Work with young people is a major strand of their practice; they are the author of *'Ask Too Much of Me'* for the NYT ensemble (Peacock Theatre 2019); *this is a room...* for Dublin Youth Theatre (Dublin Theatre Festival 2017); and ran the inaugural ARTICULATE programme for young writers for Youth Theatre Ireland 2020–2023. They are the librettist, with Annemarie NíChuirreáin, of Michael Gallen's opera *Elsewhere*, which premiered on the Abbey Stage in 2021, and the sole librettist of *Horse Ape Bird*, an INO and Music Generation cocommission, by David Coonan. They contributed text to THISISPOPBABY's queer cabaret extravaganza *WAKE*. They were the facilitator of the inaugural WEFT Studio Group, a peer mentorship and support network for Black artists and artists of colour more broadly.

Other Titles in this Series

Chris Bush
THE ASSASSINATION OF KATIE HOPKINS
   with Matt Winkworth
THE CHANGING ROOM
CHRIS BUSH PLAYS: ONE
A DOLL'S HOUSE *after* Ibsen
FAUSTUS: THAT DAMNED WOMAN
HUNGRY
JANE EYRE *after* Brontë
THE LAST NOËL
OTHERLAND
ROBIN HOOD AND THE
   CHRISTMAS HEIST
   with Matt Winkworth
ROCK / PAPER / SCISSORS
STANDING AT THE SKY'S EDGE
   with Richard Hawley
STEEL

Caryl Churchill
BLUE HEART
CHURCHILL PLAYS: THREE
CHURCHILL PLAYS: FOUR
CHURCHILL PLAYS: FIVE
CHURCHILL: SHORTS
CLOUD NINE
DING DONG THE WICKED
A DREAM PLAY *after* Strindberg
DRUNK ENOUGH TO SAY I LOVE YOU?
ESCAPED ALONE
FAR AWAY
GLASS. KILL. BLUEBEARD'S FRIENDS.
   IMP.
HERE WE GO
HOTEL
ICECREAM
LIGHT SHINING IN BUCKINGHAMSHIRE
LOVE AND INFORMATION
MAD FOREST
A NUMBER
PIGS AND DOGS
SEVEN JEWISH CHILDREN
THE SKRIKER
THIS IS A CHAIR
THYESTES *after* Seneca
TRAPS
WHAT IF IF ONLY

Carys D. Coburn
CITYSONG AND OTHER PLAYS
MALAPROP: PLAYS
   with MALAPROP Theatre

Caitríona Daly
DUCK DUCK GOOSE
THE LUNCH PUNCH POWER HOUR
   IN CONFERENCE ROOM 4

Nancy Harris
THE BEACON
NO ROMANCE
OUR NEW GIRL
THE RED SHOES
SOMEWHERE OUT THERE YOU
TWO LADIES

David Horan
CLASS *with* Iseult Golden
SANDPAPER ON SUNBURN

Deirdre Kinahan
CROSSINGS
DEIRDRE KINAHAN: SHORTS
HALCYON DAYS
MOMENT
RAGING: THREE PLAYS/SEVEN YEARS
   OF WARFARE IN IRELAND
RATHMINES ROAD
THE SAVIOUR
SPINNING
THE UNMANAGEABLE SISTERS
   after Michel Tremblay

Lucy Kirkwood
BEAUTY AND THE BEAST
   with Katie Mitchell
BLOODY WIMMIN
THE CHILDREN
CHIMERICA
HEDDA *after* Ibsen
THE HUMAN BODY
IT FELT EMPTY WHEN THE HEART
   WENT AT FIRST BUT IT IS
   ALRIGHT NOW
LUCY KIRKWOOD PLAYS: ONE
MOSQUITOES
NSFW
RAPTURE
TINDERBOX
THE WELKIN

Jack Thorne
2ND MAY 1997
AFTER LIFE *after* Hirokazu Kore-eda
BUNNY
BURYING YOUR BROTHER IN
   THE PAVEMENT
A CHRISTMAS CAROL *after* Dickens
THE END OF HISTORY…
HOPE
JACK THORNE PLAYS: ONE
JACK THORNE PLAYS: TWO
JUNKYARD
LET THE RIGHT ONE IN
   after John Ajvide Lindqvist
THE MOTIVE AND THE CUE
MYDIDAE
THE SOLID LIFE OF SUGAR WATER
STACY & FANNY AND FAGGOT
WHEN WINSTON WENT TO WAR WITH
   THE WIRELESS
WHEN YOU CURE ME
WOYZECK *after* Büchner

debbie tucker green
BORN BAD
DEBBIE TUCKER GREEN PLAYS: ONE
DIRTY BUTTERFLY
EAR FOR EYE
HANG
NUT
A PROFOUNDLY AFFECTIONATE,
   PASSIONATE DEVOTION TO
   SOMEONE (– *NOUN*)
RANDOM
STONING MARY
TRADE & GENERATIONS
TRUTH AND RECONCILIATION

Carys D. Coburn

BÁN
&
ABSENT
THE WRONG

NICK HERN BOOKS
London
www.nickhernbooks.co.uk

A Nick Hern Book

BÁN & Absent The Wrong: Two Plays first published in Great Britain in 2025 as a paperback original by Nick Hern Books Limited, The Glasshouse, 49a Goldhawk Road, London W12 8QP

BÁN & Absent The Wrong: Two Plays copyright © 2025 Carys D. Coburn

Carys D. Coburn has asserted their right to be identified as the author of this work

Front cover: photograph of Malua Ní Chléirigh, Liadán Dunlea, Bebhinn Hunt-Sheridan, Bláithín Mac Gabhann, Niamh McCann by Patricio Cassinoni

Designed and typeset by Nick Hern Books, London
Printed in Great Britain by Mimeo Ltd, Huntingdon, Cambridgeshire PE29 6XX

A CIP catalogue record for this book is available from the British Library

ISBN 978 1 83904 483 0

CAUTION All rights whatsoever in these plays are strictly reserved. Requests to reproduce the text in whole or in part should be addressed to the publisher. This book may not be used, in whole or in part, for the development or training of artificial intelligence technologies or systems.

Amateur Performing Rights Applications for performance, including readings and excerpts, by amateurs in the English language throughout the world should be addressed to the Performing Rights Manager, Nick Hern Books, The Glasshouse, 49a Goldhawk Road, London W12 8QP, *tel* +44 (0)20 8749 4953, *email* rights@nickhernbooks.co.uk, except as follows:

Australia: ORiGiN Theatrical, *email* enquiries@originmusic.com.au, *web* www.origintheatrical.com.au

New Zealand: Play Bureau, 20 Rua Street, Mangapapa, Gisborne, 4010, *tel* +64 21 258 3998, *email* info@playbureau.com

Professional Performing Rights Applications for performance by professionals in any medium and in any language throughout the world should be addressed to Independent Talent Group Ltd, 40 Whitfield Street, London W1T 2RH, *tel* +44 (0)20 7636 6565

No performance of any kind may be given unless a licence has been obtained. Applications should be made before rehearsals begin. Publication of these plays does not necessarily indicate their availability for amateur performance.

www.nickhernbooks.co.uk/environmental-policy

Nick Hern Books' authorised representative in the EU is
Easy Access System Europe – Mustamäe tee 50, 10621 Tallinn, Estonia
email gpsr.requests@easproject.com

World Premiere
An Abbey Theatre production

BÁN
Written by Carys D. Coburn

An Abbey Theatre commission

First performed on 30 September 2025 at the Abbey Theatre, Dublin

CAST
Bernadette	Bríd Ní Neachtain
Frances	Yvonne Gidden
Mary Elizabeth	Niamh McCann
Mary Louise	Bláithín Mac Gabhann
Annie	Malua Ní Chléirigh
Mary Rose	Bebhinn Hunt-Sheridan
Edele	Liadán Dunlea

CREATIVES
Playwright	Carys D. Coburn
Director	Claire O'Reilly
Set and Costume Designer	Sarah Bacon
Lighting Designer	Lee Curran
Composer and Sound Designer	Jenny O'Malley
Dramaturg	Ruth McGowan
Voice Director	Cathal Quinn
Movement Director	Gabrielle Moleta
Fight Director	Ciarán O'Grady
Hair and Make Up	Tee Elliott
Casting Director	Barry Coyle
Assistant Director	Úna Nolan

COMPANY
Senior Producer	Craig Flaherty
Producer	Cally Shine
Production Manager	Andy Keogh
Production Coordinator	Justin Murphy
Assistant Producer	Aoife McCollum
Company Manager	Danny Erskine
Company Stage Manager	Clive Welsh
Deputy Stage Manager	Roxzan Bowes
Assistant Stage Manager	Aidan Doheny
Head of Costume & Costume Hire	Donna Geraghty
Costume Supervisor	Yvonne Kelly
Props Master	Eimer Murphy
Props Supervisor	Adam O'Connell
Head of Lighting and Sound	Kevin McFadden

Lighting Operations Manager	Simon Burke
Sound Operations Manager	Morgan Dunne
Sound Supervisor	Derek Conaghy
Marketing	Muireann Kane, John Tierney
Publicity	Mia O'Reilly
Digital Engagement	Eva Louise O'Beirne
Publicity Image	Patricio Cassinoni
Irish Sign Language Interpreters	Caoimhe Coburn Gray, Vanessa O'Connell
Artistic Director/Co-Director	Caitríona McLaughlin
Executive Director/Co-Director	Mark O'Brien

THE ABBEY THEATRE

As Ireland's national theatre, the Abbey Theatre's ambition is to enrich the cultural lives of everyone with a curiosity for and interest in Irish theatre, stories, artists and culture. Courage and imagination are at the heart of our storytelling, while inclusivity, diversity and equality are at the core of our thinking. Led by Co-Directors Caitríona McLaughlin (Artistic Director) and Mark O'Brien (Executive Director), the Abbey Theatre celebrates both the rich canon of Irish dramatic writing and the potential of future generations of Irish theatre artists.

Ireland has a rich history of theatre and playwriting and extraordinary actors, designers and directors. Artists are at the heart of our organisation, with Marina Carr and Conor McPherson as Senior Associate Playwrights and Caroline Byrne as Associate Director.

Our stories teach us what it is to belong, what it is to be excluded and to exclude. Artistically our programme is built on twin impulses, and around two questions: 'who we were, and who are we now?' We interrogate our classical canon with an urgency about what makes it speak to this moment. On our stages we find and champion new voices and new ways of seeing, our purpose – to identify combinations of characters we are yet to meet, having conversations we are yet to hear.

abbeytheatre.ie

ABBEY THEATRE SUPPORTERS

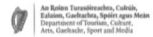

funding theatre (arts council / ealaíon)

OLLSCOIL NA GAILLIMHE / UNIVERSITY OF GALWAY

An Roinn Turasóireachta, Cultúir, Ealaíon, Gaeltachta, Spóirt agus Meán / Department of Tourism, Culture, Arts, Gaeltacht, Sport and Media

PROGRAMME PARTNER
RTÉ arts

EDUCATION PARTNER
UNIVERSITY OF NOTRE DAME | KYLEMORE

CORPORATE GUARDIANS
Bloomberg   THE IRISH TIMES
Irish Life   NORTHERN TRUST   ESB

ASSOCIATE ACCESS PARTNER
Vhi

GOLD AMBASSADORS
Ipsos B&A   ecclesiastical
FLYNN HODKINSON   Lindt EXCELLENCE
McCann FitzGerald

RETAIL PARTNER
ARNOTTS

HOSPITALITY PARTNER
THE WESTBURY
THE DOYLE COLLECTION · DUBLIN

IT PARTNER
Qualcom

SILVER AMBASSADOR
interpath   ODGERS BERNDTSON
wines direct

RESTAURANT PARTNERS
DOLIER STREET   DUNNE & CRESCENZI
HAWKSMOOR   NANNETTI'S
CUCINA ITALIANA

PLAYWRIGHT DEVELOPMENT PARTNER
O'Neill Family

GUARDIANS
The Cielinski Family
Deirdre and Irial Finan
Carmel and Martin Naughton
Sheelagh O'Neill
Donal Moore R.I.P.
John and Sarah Reynolds

VISIONARIES
Tony Ahearne
Pat and Kate Butler
Leisha Daly
Janice Flynn

INNOVATORS
Gerard and Liv McNaughton
Louise Richardson R.I.P.

CHAMPION
Tommy Gibbons
Eugene Magee
Andrew and Delyth Parkes

CREATORS
Frances Britton
Rory Dwyer
Margaret Roohan
Charles J. Young

EXPLORERS
Valerie Cole
Thelma Doran
Peter Howlett
Kathy Hutton
Mary and Kevin Hoy
John Gabriel Irwin
Anne Lardener
Janet O'Brien
Tina Robinson
Kathleen Walsh

We want to thank the listed supporters for their ongoing generosity and belief in Ireland's National Theatre. We would also like to thank our generous supporters who have asked to remain anonymous. .

BÁN

After Lorca

Why Adapt? Why Lorca? Why Bernarda? Why '*BÁN*'?

If you play a lot of video games, you probably know what reskinning is. It's when you take a game that already exists and make it look different – different colour scheme, different character sprites, different names for attacks, items, equipment – without substantially altering its fundamental logic. Fans do it for fun. *I want to play* Skyrim, *but I want all the dragons to be Thomas the Tank Engine*. Corporations do it for profit. *Why make a new game when we could just do* Skyrim *in Space?*

You can approach adapting a play this way. You can replace every *drat* with a *fuck*, every rouble with a euro, every noble with a financier, you can transpose from ancient Athens to present-day Drumshanbo. It can be fun, and sometimes these transpositions generate moments of surprise that bring something into focus in the parent work. *Oh! I never saw that that way.* But frequently, I think, superficial changes generate only superficial insights.

In music there's a term for a piece that mirrors the harmonic or melodic structure of another – it's called a contrafact. Miles Davis's 'Tune-Up', despite its name, falls and then rises; John Coltrane's 'Countdown', despite its name, rises and then falls. 'Tune-Up' cycles between three keys, and it takes four bars to do so each time; 'Countdown' accelerates the cycle, makes it denser and wilder, the harmony changing three times for each of 'Tune-Up's three changes. But somehow, magically, almost like Coltrane planned it, every phrase of 'Countdown' ends in the same key as each phrase in 'Tune-Up'. Miles Davis shows us a rainbow of three stripes – John Coltrane interposes clouds of notes between us and that rainbow, but every so often they're swept away and it shines through.

I prefer contrafacts to reskins in adaptation. You could call it the Cordelia approach, more faithful to the parent in defiance. Or the Beethoven approach – when classical language doesn't fit any more you take it apart at the seams, quilt it into a jacket or a blanket, some reconstellated shape that can serve you some other way. The challenge is to treat the original as a dare rather than a target. Can I go faster here without falling? Can I open this gap wider without making it uncrossable? Can I connect these points without short-circuiting the flow of energy and blowing the whole thing up?

Literalising the idea of the parent work, imagine how an adult and child cross rocks on a beach. Where the elder picks their way, the younger jumps. Where the elder looks ahead, the younger plunges in. For neither is the route practical – for both, the pleasure is in the traversal of terrain that challenges you. But the child's pleasures are other, wilder.

Lorca's plays, rich landscapes of contradictions and provocations, lyricism alongside realism alongside soap opera alongside politics, invite this kind of traversal. They're karst, so no two people crossing the riven surface take the same route. There is a contrived point to make here about karst being a landscape common to Ireland and Andalusia, with El Torcal de Antequera about as far from Lorca's birthplace as the Burren is from Cork. But I distrust the idea that origins are explanations, that landscape is destiny, that blood and soil are siblings. The key thing with karst is how it makes you move. The number of possible paths is the factorial of the number of islands. The question is not what *can* this play say, it's what *can't* it?

For example: it is deeply strange to me that the lyrical Lorca is canonised and the political Lorca is marginalised. Yes, okay, The Moon gets a lovely monologue in *Blood Wedding* – a play about the irreconcilable demands of passion and property. Famously, Fred scanned the papers for stories of *duende*, human interest with teeth, desire leading to death or vice versa. But if duende is just intensity of feeling why not invent it? Why does pure shining emotion need footnotes, accreditation in smeary newsprint?

Unless the smears are the points. He wanted the adversity, the perversity, the banal given from which something radically other blooms, falters, dies. Roses growing in middens. Passion drives a Lorca play, but it rarely wins. That fact has a political charge. It says something about the weight of history, the difficulty of becoming otherwise. I'm being etymologically literal when I say *passion* rather than *desire*, because a passion is a desire that hurts. Passion is the want that calls our sense of self into question – *who am I, if I want this?*

If I try to say what THE Lorca mood or gesture is, the quandary his characters face time and time again, I land on a question: How to be fully human in a world that doesn't want you to be? How to live a life where you don't just recite your assigned lines, where you are more than a cog in the machine of the family or the town or the state? *Yerma* feels dated if you stage it as a quest, if Yerma 'just' wants a child because children are wonderful, motherhood is wonderful, so she's chasing them as fast as she can. But if *mother* is the only alternative to *wife*, and *wife* is unbearable, then we're in a rich paradox – to escape one womanhood, I dive into another. There is a choice, but there is no good choice. That's the Lorca I wanted to adapt.

When I started working on my version of *The House of Bernarda Alba*, I had been reading a lot about the family. Not kinship, and not blood – kinship doesn't require blood, and the family denies blood as often as not. The family is a set of laws, some enforced by the state and some by its members. *Fathers aren't guardians automatically even if they're named on the birth cert. Don't mention your brother's hairline.* When the family is working everyone knows their place, their duties and entitlements, what they own or owe. This has never happened. A stable family is nearly a contradiction in terms, because all too easily it tips over into too many people inheriting too little or too few people managing too much. This applies whether it's a house or attention, wealth or love, at issue.

Think of those staples of the nineteenth-century novel: the wealthy widow or widower in search of a suitable heir, and the orphan in search of a suitable family. It's comic in *Oliver Twist* and *Nicholas Nickleby*; ironised in *Bleak House* and *Great Expectations*. The wealthy widow or widower's predicament unites the two problems of family; no primary line, too many secondary claimants. Scarcity and excess side by side, neither serving anyone. A productive paradox – that the family, like an empire, must sustain itself by dispersing itself. We need a child to inherit; they might die, so better have some spares; oh shit, we have all these spare children, better marry off the daughters and put the sons to work; oh shit, our sons are getting people pregnant faster than we can marry off our daughters, better declare some of these children illegitimate; oh shit, we're giving away more in dowries than we're gaining in property, better lower the wages in the factory or lengthen the hours or steal our neighbour's land and force them to work for us...

No wonder family drama looms so large for playwrights. Family is a machine that is supposed to produce stability, continuity, love, and instead it gives us chaos, estrangement, abuse. We can't survive without the support of our family, but it's not enough to sustain us by itself. The people who are supposed to love us hurt us, or do love us but in every way except the way we need. The ironies are as painful as they are rich.

Lorca's plays have a holy trinity at their heart: family, land, purity. You can't continue the family without the land; you can't inherit the land unless you're pure; you can only be pure if you belong to the family. Passion is the force that derails this circular train, makes it jump its tracks. Force is required to return it to its orderly procession – force isn't necessarily violence, force can be offered money or looming starvation, but in Lorca it is often violence. This too tells a truth, that we don't live this way by choice. We will be punished if we don't.

Lorca, in writing about this kind of rural land politics, was writing about the world of his parents. When I write about Ireland in the eighties I am doing the same. I don't live there, but it casts a long shadow in my life. The last line of Lorca's *The House of Bernarda Alba* is 'She died pure'. Bernarda's family name, 'Alba', means *dawn* via a root that means *white*. I find that connection rich.

My mother is not white, but she was raised thinking she was. Religious orders decreed it better for children to grow up with stable (white) married (white) parents, whatever they were like, even if it came at the cost of any connection to their heritage. The state deemed it fit that married women give birth in hospitals whose sheets were cleaned by unmarried women in laundries. And the Association of Mixed Race Irish's shadow report to the UN's Committee on the Elimination of Racial Discrimination marshalls the evidence that mixed-race children were dispreferred for adoption, by the agencies notionally caring for them if not prospective parents. Meaning they were more likely to spend their early lives in institutions, more likely to lack the family networks of care that could keep people out of those institutions in adult life. The Irish family is white and nuclear by fiat, not in fact. This too is force. As is lying – *sorry, we have no records pertaining to your birth family. No, we don't know why you look so different from your siblings.* So not only does it take force to keep the (white) family on track, it takes force to found it in the first place.

The image of those clean sheets, cleaned by prisoners, is particularly hard for me to shake. Maybe it's because the image and its production tell such different stories. Behind purity, brutality. Maybe because I was born in the Rotunda. If I'm cycling to work nearby or to visit my mother, I pass the Sean McDermott Street Laundry. It's less than five minutes from hospital to laundry on a bike. It was still open the year I was born, so the question looms. And, writing this, I realise one of the central images of *BÁN* is bloodied sheets. An attempt to harmonise appearance and essence, perhaps. *BÁN* was written as a companion to *Absent The Wrong*, the other play in this collection, which delves into all of this history. *BÁN* isn't as explicit in dealing with it, but its roots are as firmly planted in it. It concerns itself with a single household rather than the state, whose occupants don't want to be there but are terrified to leave. *Absent The Wrong* is about all the reasons the characters in *BÁN* had to be terrified; *BÁN* keeps a tight focus on how terror makes us treat one another.

I read *The House of Bernarda Alba* as a kind of gothic drama. *BÁN* certainly is. One way of thinking about the gothic is that it is preoccupied with the impossibility of purity, the high cost incurred in pursuit of it, often paid in blood. It is a genre where our present hopes and dreams founder on the past. Debts incurred prior to our birth upstage all our projects, our very best intentions. The good suffer in spite of their goodness; the bad suffer irrespective of their badness. We can scrub ourselves raw but we will still not be clean, or not for long – some wrong will be disinterred, thrust into our hands, leaving us muddied or bloodied. Sometimes this is literal. The second act of Lorca's play ends with dogs digging up a murdered baby, and the people of the town lynching its unmarried mother. His Bernarda calls for the mob to put *burning coal in the place of her sin*. I will leave you to find out how I handled this in the context of eighties Ireland, saying only that precedents and echoes were not hard to find.

Sometimes a lot of emphasis is put on the supernatural's role in the gothic, but a more abstracted definition would say that ghosts and monsters are just one tool for mortifying the understanding. It looks to the gothic protagonist like the rules of reality are being broken; in a happy gothic ending they realise that they were wrong, that those ghostly voices were just servants behind the wall; in an unhappy gothic ending, arguably more in the spirit of the project, it turns out that what you believed to be the rules weren't broken because they never obtained in the first place.

Every character in *BÁN* makes at least one bad decision. Most of them are made during the play, but a few big ones pre-exist the action. If the world were fair, then the bad results of those decisions would be proportional to the error. But the sisters' bad decisions domino into their mother's, so that all unknowing they tip themselves into a downward spiral they can't escape. There's a lot of talk from everyone about getting square, making things right at last, as if by saying it is so they can make it so. But a gothic world isn't transactional. There can be no return to a tit-for-tat universe for them, because these characters never lived there.

My favourite gothic works all belong to its regional branches. Not the works from the heart of empire, where blood seeps up out of the ground and stains the Great Work. I prefer the gothic when we begin disillusioned, where there is no melancholic attachment to what was lost. *Isn't Mr Rochester dreamy? If only he hadn't had that Creole wife…* I grew up on North Strand – I spent my teens cycling past the Archbishop's Palace in Drumcondra on the way to my grandparents', the hundreds of shoes tied to the railing. It was a familiar sight by the time I thought to ask what it meant. *Oh.* The reveal not of what was hidden, but of what was in plain sight and couldn't yet be fully grasped. That's a classic gesture for the strain of gothic I prefer.

Wide Sargasso Sea is an easy example, with its parent work kept in view. Or you could cite Faulkner here, *Absalom, Absalom!* or *Go Down, Moses*, the unease at the heart of plantation life for white people surrounded by Black half-brothers and sisters and aunts and uncles and cousins they can't acknowledge without acknowledging that their own privilege is rooted in obscenity. The gothic irony, that your power not only does not permit you to speak your mind but demands your silence – provided you want to keep it, that is. Or Arundhati Roy's *The God of Small Things*, a perfect gothic novel working with all of the gothic's great preoccupations: incest, the regime of race (here in the form of caste), haunted houses where the past is more vivid than the present.

Why incest and why race? Werner Sollors, in *Neither Black Nor White Yet Both: Thematic Explorations of Interracial Literature*, says that for the institution of the family, incest and miscegenation are complementary dooms. (And the gothic, of course, loves a good doom. Why settle for destroying an individual when you can destroy their whole line?) Both incest and miscegenation threaten the downfall of the line of inheritance, one by sticking 'too close' and one by straying 'too far'. The nineteenth-century gothic often treats race as a kind of original sin – mad Creole Bertha, angry swarthy Heathcliff, bestial Romanian (bisexual?) Dracula. The rules for vampires are generalisable to all racial others – *Don't invite them in, or we'll be destroyed!* But remember that it takes force, violence, to found the family as well as to preserve it. The twentieth-century post-colonial gothic more often begins from this vantage, not mourning the purity lost but showing what it cost in the first place. It shows us race as the regime it is, rather than presumptive biological fact. It shows that if incest is the acme of racial purity, and it is a crime, then the (white) family's preservation is its damnation. In other words: purity is death.

Which brings me back to the final line of Lorca's play – 'she died pure'. I kept a version of it in *BÁN*. I said that I have tried to retraverse the terrain of Lorca's play; if *The House of Bernarda Alba* is about denial, *BÁN* is about delusion. It steers into the skid of the parent play, because delusion is denial carried past the point of reason. Even when a belief can no longer give you anything, when it no longer makes it easier to face the day or your boss or the truth, you cling to it. Maybe because, as long as you're clinging to it, it can't be said that you have nothing. When the play begins some of the characters are both deceived and deluded; they don't understand the life they're living because they haven't been given the chance. By the end all are undeceived, but some are still deluded. They still think wanting something to be true can make it true. They still think they can force it to be true. And *BÁN* charts the price they all pay for that delusion.

Carys D. Coburn,
September 2025

'A pair of actors trapped in a recondite play with no hint of plot or narrative. Stumbling through their parts, nursing someone else's sorrows. Grieving someone else's grief. Unable, somehow, to change plays. Or purchase, for a fee, some cheap brand of exorcism... But anger wasn't available to them and there was no face to put on this Other Thing that they held in their sticky Other Hands, like an imaginary orange. There was nowhere to lay it down. It wasn't theirs to give away. It would have to be held. Carefully and forever.'

Arundhati Roy, The God of Small Things

'Let me tell you a secret: people get really angry when you suggest to them that they deserved better than what they got growing up. And I've noticed that a lot of people have the "but I love my family" reaction with the most startling vehemence immediately after they've spent a long time talking freely to me about the strain, tragedy, blackmail, and care-starved frustration that characterized their "biological" upbringing...

Listen. I get it. It's not just that you're worried about your dad getting all upset if he sees you with this book. It's that it's existentially petrifying to imagine relinquishing the organized poverty we have in favor of an abundance we have never known and have yet to organize.'

Sophie Lewis, Abolish the Family:
A Manifesto for Care and Liberation

'If we understand whiteness as the systematic denial of being in relation, in particular to Black and Indigenous people, we can ask what being in right relations, relations of reciprocity, could mean or look like. White treason is a way to claim kin. We can only be treasonous to something we claim, or that claims us.'

Alexis Shotwell, Claiming Bad Kin

'Slavery is the ghost in the machine of kinship. Kinship relations structure the nation. Capitulation to their current configurations is the continued enfleshment of that ghost.'

Christina Sharpe, Lose Your Kin

Characters

BERNADETTE (BERNIE), *sixties. She is white*

FRANCES, *sixties. Bernadette's sister. She is Black. Unlike the other Black character in the play, she knows it*

MARY ELIZABETH (LIZZY), *forty. Bernadette's daughter. She is white*

MARY LOUISE, *thirty. Mary Elizabeth's sister. She is white*

ANNETTE (ANNIE), *twenty-seven. Mary Louise's sister. She is Black, even if she wouldn't or couldn't self-describe that way when the play takes place. Heavily pregnant when the play begins*

MARY ROSE, *twenty-four. Annie's sister. She is white and she is Deaf/hard of hearing, even if she wouldn't or couldn't self-describe that way when the play takes place*

EDELE, *twenty. Mary Rose's sister. She is white*

Note on Text

– on a line by itself indicates a beat/change of intention, not necessarily a huge pause.

/ indicates an overlap point, after which the following line can come in.

/ A line surrounded by overlaps / is spoken over, either by the preceding line or the following line as context demands.

Square brackets [] indicate the intended/possible completion of an inconclusive line – just in case you need it.

Bold text is directed to the audience.

Note on Play

The play takes place in Ireland, some time in the middle of the 1980s, in a house a respectable distance outside a town. The town is in Cork unless there's a fantastic reason it shouldn't be. I've given castings/character experiences in contemporary parlance, though, because you'll be staging the play in the present. Those experiences should be represented in the rehearsal room – ideally in both the cast and the creative team.

This text went to press before the end of rehearsals and so may differ slightly from the play as performed.

ACT ONE

The kitchen before the funeral. No table. MARY ELIZABETH (LIZZY), MARY LOUISE, MARY ROSE, ANNETTE (ANNIE) *and* EDELE *are making sandwiches on a wooden board on top of a Servis twin-tub top-loader washing machine that would have been a serious showpiece a few decades back. The washing machine is on, vibrating hard, in a way that makes it hard for the sisters to make neat tidy funeral-ready sandwiches. The washing machine might actually move across the floor, if this can be pulled off without bankrupting the production. Someone might nearly overbalance the entire set-up by pressing too hard without a hard surface underneath them, provided it doesn't feel forced or become a whole affair. We hold on sandwich-making for a long moment.* ANNIE, *it bears mentioning, is visibly/heavily pregnant.*

LOUISE (*with every intention of leading her sisters in a decade of the rosary, precedent notwithstanding*). The first sorrowful mystery, / the agony in the garden

LIZZY. / Ah Lou /

ANNIE. / Don't Louise /

EDELE. / NO thank you, NO prayers today, stop RIGHT now, thanks /

LOUISE *subsides. They make sandwiches.*

LIZZY. I was just thinking there about how Claude ('*Cloud.*') Lévi-Strauss said, or, / wrote actually

LOUISE. / Please /

ANNIE. / Don't Lizzy /

EDELE. / NO, ABSOLUTELY NOT /

LIZZY *subsides. They make sandwiches.* ROSE *steps away from making sandwiches.*

ROSE

ACT ONE   17

ROSE *goes to the radio.*

/ ROSE /

ANNIE. / Let her /

ROSE *turns on the radio and turns the volume way up before starting to look for a station she wants.*

LIZZY. / ROSE /

ANNIE. / ROSE, pet, it's a bit loud /

LOUISE. / She can't hear you, she hasn't got her hearing aids in, she never does /

EDELE. / FIND THE STATION FIRST, THEN TURN IT UP, HOW MANY FUCKING TIMES ROSE /

ROSE

EDELE *waves, trying to catch* ROSE's *attention.*

ROSE

EDELE *takes a piece of ham from the table and throws it at* ROSE. *If she misses, she continues saying her name louder and louder and throwing ham until it hits* ROSE, *getting her attention. At some point in the following before the radio gets turned off, the radio should land on 'There's No One Quite Like Grandma' – causing all the previously neutral/ bystanding/pro-appeasement sisters to come over to* EDELE's *anti-radio position.*

ROSE. What?

EDELE. TURN IT DOWN

ROSE. I can't hear it if it's not loud

EDELE (*not hearing her over the radio*). WHAT?

ANNIE *waves to get* ROSE's *attention.*

ANNIE. [speak] LOUDER ROSE

ROSE. THE RADIO [should be louder]?

ROSE *turns the radio up even louder, to general disapproval.*

EDELE. ABSOLUTELY NOT THE RADIO

ANNIE. <u>SPEAK</u> LOUDER ROSE

EDELE. AND TURN THE RADIO <u>DOWN</u>

ROSE. I CAN'T HEAR IT IF IT'S NOT LOUD

EDELE. SO PUT IN YOUR FUCKING HEARING AIDS

ROSE. THE BATTERY'S NEARLY GONE

EDELE. AND IT WOULD BE <u>SO</u> TERRIBLE IF THEY DIED AND YOU COULDN'T HEAR AND WE HAD TO SHOUT

During the preceding, EDELE *has crossed the room to turn down the radio – and* FRANCES *has entered. Acknowledgement from all except* LIZZY.

ROSE. I'm BORED

EDELE. And I'm not?

FRANCES. You'll have the woman herself in now

LIZZY. She told us no music, / she told us

EDELE. You're such a lick

LOUISE. Ah leave her Edèle

FRANCES. She loves that one, is what I meant

EDELE. Which is funny

FRANCES. Why?

EDELE. Is it funny?

LOUISE. Ah Edele

FRANCES. Yeah

EDELE. Not exactly delighted Annie's making her a grandmother, is she

LIZZY. EDELE

ANNIE. It's fine, it's, is she – [upstairs]?

FRANCES. She's out on the road

ACT ONE   19

LIZZY. Why is she out in the road?

LOUISE. Looking for Davitt from the funeral home

FRANCES *inspects the sandwiches.*

FRANCES. Ham?

ANNIE. And egg

FRANCES. Ham and egg?

LIZZY. There's ham and cheese and there's egg as well

LOUISE. I hate egg

FRANCES. Just egg?

LIZZY. Egg salad

FRANCES. Butter?

ANNIE. Loads

ANNIE *hands* FRANCES *an egg sandwich.*

LIZZY. Those are for the guests

FRANCES. The guests?

LOUISE. Mourners

LIZZY. I meant mourners

FRANCES. But you said guests

LIZZY. If you're not doing anything Frances, we could do with another thing of butter

FRANCES. That's interesting

LIZZY. And another batch [loaf] or two wouldn't do any harm

FRANCES. Tell me more

LIZZY. Just it's only yourself and myself drive

FRANCES. True

LIZZY. –

I'll go then

LIZZY *exits. The washing machine stops. General relief.*

EDELE. Thank fuck

FRANCES. I shouldn't – [say this]

ANNIE. But?

LOUISE. Don't

EDELE. Do

FRANCES. None of you saw Lizzy with the tie the other night, no?

ROSE. With the what?

ANNIE (*gesturing a tie as she speaks*). The tie for him to wear

FRANCES. Not the tie for him to wear, to close his mouth

ANNIE. Oh

ROSE. His mouth?

ANNIE. Yeah

ROSE. Was it – ?

ANNIE. Yeah?

ROSE. –

Stuck?

FRANCES. If we'd left it it would have stuck, yeah

ROSE. Ugh

FRANCES. But he's just gone, it's late, and she says we're not to call anyone until the morning but she wants his mouth closed now before anyone sees him, only we're not to use any of his ties because they're already boxed up to be given away to the St Vincent de Paul

EDELE. Her and her fucking – [Vinny de P boxes]

LOUISE. What about the one he was to wear?

FRANCES. She'd already laid it out for him

EDELE. Oh of course

FRANCES. So then Lizzy's running around like a mad thing looking for something, anything, and she's opening drawers (*Does so.*)

ACT ONE   21

EDELE. Yeah?

FRANCES. And she picks up the Sellotape and looks at it

FRANCES *demonstrates* LIZZY's *thought process until they catch on – maybe we can wrap Sellotape around our dead father's head to keep his mouth shut!*

ROSE. Oh my god

EDELE. Oh my god

LOUISE. Oh Lizzy

ANNIE. Oh no

FRANCES. And that's not even the best part

LOUISE. Ah come on

EDELE (*demanding*). What?

ROSE (*clarifying*). What?

ANNIE (*to* ROSE). There's more

LOUISE. Ah no

EDELE. That's a wind-up

FRANCES. It's not

EDELE. Go on then

FRANCES. She stops dead right here and guess what she says out loud to herself

LOUISE. Oh god

ROSE. What?

EDELE. Just tell us

FRANCES (*pointing to the washing machine*). She goes *I don't suppose the hose*, all thoughtful

ANNIE. –

She didn't

LOUISE. Christ

ROSE. The hose off the washing machine?

EDELE. OH MY GOD LIZZY

BERNADETTE (*who no one except this script would ever call* BERNIE) *enters. She dresses austerely throughout the play. She wears one unostentatious necklace throughout too.* FRANCES *and the daughters fall quiet.*

BERNIE (*to* FRANCES). Davitt is on his way with him, and the room still isn't fit to be seen

FRANCES. And when was I supposed to give it a look?

BERNIE. What's stopping you now?

FRANCES *exits, not without comment/protest/exasperation.* BERNIE *looks at her daughters.*

–

Your father is dead and soon to be buried, lying beside my first husband where I was meant to lie, and let that be the end of men for us, let us close the account at a loss before we lose everything, because man's in debt to woman for his birth, his milk, his spoon brought to his mouth, his kisses-better on his scrapes, and he hates debt because it's living on the side of a mountain, dropped cups rolling away from your fingers, sleeping with your feet above your head, never building your house fast enough and it always crumbling away, and so he marries, sputters his gruel into some poor daughter's gap as though that's the scales moved, and every drop of blood mashed into the first-night sheets is another stony field or sour orchard of dowry or brideprice or whatever the coloureds call it for some skinny scabby daughter who'll be filled by some son and have daughters who'll be filled, or some son who'll slop some daughter and have sons who'll slop, beggars and beggars and beggars and beggars until the kingdom, I say, enough, no more, we'll not disgrace ourselves further, are we blacks?

–

I said are we blacks?

ANNIE (*with absolutely no irony stemming from her own Blackness*). No Mammy

–

ACT ONE   23

BERNIE. That's the end of it now. No more beaus, no more weddings, no more children, / and the family disgrace

EDELE *laughs. Everyone else looks at her.*

What's funny then?

EDELE. Nothing

BERNIE. Then what's there to laugh about?

EDELE. Nothing

BERNIE *stares her down.* EDELE *holds her nerve.*

BERNIE. The family disgrace will end with us because the family name will end with us, and about time too

BERNIE *notices that* ROSE *isn't following as closely as she'd like, with her gaze elsewhere in the room.*

MARY ROSE?

One of her sisters nudges ROSE *to make her tune in.*

ROSE. Yeah?

BERNIE. Are you listening?

ROSE. Yes Mammy

BERNIE. So what did I just say?

ROSE. You asked me was I listening

BERNIE. Before that

ROSE. –

(*Guessing.*) About Daddy

BERNIE. What about him?

ROSE *draws a blank.* BERNIE *goes to the plate of sandwiches. She takes one and holds it up demonstratively.*

ROSE (*guessing*). Or, you were asking if we're done

With none of the earlier sense of play, BERNIE *throws a sandwich at* ROSE *– hard. Then advances on her.*

BERNIE. I won't pay for you to have hearing aids if you don't use them, do you understand? Do you understand?

ROSE. Yes Mammy

BERNIE. Where are they?

ROSE. In my room

BERNIE. Go get them

ROSE. Alright Mammy

BERNIE. NOW

> BERNIE *matches her volume with a smack – more shocking than punitive or painful, but* ROSE *jumps, exits a moment later.*

> And the rest of ye get cleaning, there's food on the floor

> BERNIE *exits. A long and ultimately unbearable moment amongst the remaining sisters.*

EDELE (*to* ANNIE, *taking the piss*). 'No Mammy'

ANNIE. What?

EDELE. You're such a lick

ANNIE. She'll wait forever for you to say something

EDELE. Because she knows she can count on you to give up, / if you didn't give up she would have to

ANNIE. / I don't give up, I get it over with, there's a difference /

LOUISE. Our father is dead

ANNIE. –

> Sorry Lou

EDELE. So?

LOUISE. So?

EDELE. Not much to miss, is there? He never talked to us unless he was backing Mammy up, and we still have Lizzy for that, Daddy's ghost walks among us wearing lipgloss

LOUISE. Jesus Edele

ACT ONE   25

ANNIE. He talked to me

LOUISE. And me

EDELE. When you were doing his typing, yeah, but he just talked about his favourite records right? And you're not denying he never spoke to me or Rosie, are you? (*To* LOUISE *more than* ANNIE.) Are you going to miss him?

–

You hesitated! It's all coming out now!

LOUISE. If I say no will you stop fighting?

EDELE. Who's fighting? All I did was laugh

ANNIE. She wouldn't have gone after Rose like that if you hadn't

EDELE. It was FUNNY, she's going on about no more children and you're there with Joe Sugrue's / baby ready to fall out of you any day now, bump the size of Kilimanjaro

ANNIE. / I don't want to talk about Joe /

EDELE. My question is / what's wrong with the rest of you you DIDN'T laugh

LOUISE. / Ah Edele come on /

EDELE. Tell me straight out it wasn't funny, go on, say no Edele, it wasn't funny

BERNIE *re-enters with* FRANCES. *Everyone falls silent.*

BERNIE. What wasn't funny?

EDELE. A joke I told

BERNIE. Today?

EDELE. I wasn't thinking

BERNIE. Go on then

EDELE. I forget now

BERNIE. In the last ten seconds?

EDELE. Yeah

BERNIE. –

(*Meaning sandwiches.*) Is that all ye have done?

ANNIE. We ran out of bread

BERNIE. So you're just standing here?

LOUISE. Lizzy went to the shops already, Mammy

BERNIE. And is there drink?

ANNIE. For the mourners?

EDELE. There's a bottle of port and a bottle of gin and a half-bottle of Blue Nun

FRANCES. Which is mine anyway

BERNIE. I won't have people saying we're tight with anything

LOUISE. I'll go get more

EDELE. I'll go too

BERNIE. And you'll come straight back

EDELE. Where else would we go?

BERNIE gives EDELE one last long look, which EDELE returns, then exits. EDELE and LOUISE follow. ANNIE and FRANCES are left alone.

FRANCES. They should have asked what they're to get, what exactly, because now whatever it is it'll be wrong and she'll make them go back

Over the preceding, FRANCES has looked for and found a dustpan/broom/hoover/DustBuster/duster or equivalent. She holds it up triumphantly to ANNIE, who doesn't respond. Which occasions:

Everything alright, pet?

ANNIE. Yes!

FRANCES. You sure?

ANNIE. Just, my feet hurt

FRANCES. Then sit down

ANNIE. She might come in

FRANCES. And if she does, and if she gives you grief, I'll strangle her with the hose off the machine

–

(*As in, no laugh.*) No?

ANNIE. I had my bath last night, and I felt fine, I feel fine, but when I was getting dressed again I saw there was blood, / and it's not like I've never had, or

FRANCES. Right, well, definitely sit down

ANNIE *sits*.

ANNIE. It's not like that's new I mean, but it's been months now and at this stage isn't that really bad?

FRANCES. Just one second now before we panic, there was blood on your clothes?

ANNIE. Yeah

FRANCES. Your underwear?

ANNIE. Yeah

FRANCES. Little spots?

ANNIE. It, what's little?

FRANCES. As in, individual spots and not a big stain?

ANNIE. Then yeah

FRANCES. It was like that?

ANNIE. Yeah

FRANCES. But you felt alright?

ANNIE. Fine

FRANCES. Not light-headed, even, after the bath?

ANNIE. No

FRANCES. And your feet, I know they hurt but are they swollen?

ANNIE. A bit, but that's normal right?

FRANCES. Very normal, and any headache at all?

ANNIE. Before I go to sleep some nights

FRANCES. And does your vision go blurry?

ANNIE. No

FRANCES. Never?

ANNIE. Not yet anyway

FRANCES takes ANNIE's hand and squeezes it. Tender? Medical? Ambiguously both?

FRANCES. Right, well, good news

ANNIE. Yeah?

FRANCES. That's normal enough, it might be nothing

ANNIE. Might be?

FRANCES. As in, I saw it a lot in London and most of the time it was nothing

ANNIE. Right

FRANCES. I'll have a word with herself about you seeing the doctor

ANNIE. She doesn't want anyone to know

FRANCES. She doesn't want you to be sick either

FRANCES has grabbed a sandwich from the platter and gives it to ANNIE.

Eat something

ANNIE takes the sandwich. During the following, FRANCES locates the bottle of port and pours herself a (very) large nerve-settling glass.

ANNIE. These are for the mourners

FRANCES. You're mourning your father, aren't you?

ANNIE. –

I'm not sure about that

FRANCES. Give it time, you're in shock still

ANNIE. No I'm sad, I didn't, I meant she told me I'm not to go

FRANCES. To the church?

ACT ONE   29

ANNIE. And I'm to stay in my room when people are here

–

So no one sees me

FRANCES. –

We'll fucking see about that

ANNIE. As though they don't know already

FRANCES. We'll fucking see

ANNIE. It's fine

FRANCES. No it's not, and I'm surprised at her

ANNIE. Not me, but it does make me wonder

FRANCES. At her?

ANNIE. Or it reminds me that I used to, wonder I mean, if he really was my father

FRANCES. –

You're a changeling, are you?

ANNIE. You know what I mean

FRANCES. And I know I was there when you were born, I saw your father hold you, I saw him happier than I'd ever seen him

ANNIE. Yeah?

FRANCES. His joke was always that the only things worth crying over were the hurling and the music of Richard Wagner, but he might have shed a tear that time too

ANNIE. –

So you'd come home by then?

FRANCES. Because your mother needed the help, yeah

ANNIE. And you didn't miss nursing?

FRANCES. No I did, but some kinds of help only some people can give

ANNIE. Family

FRANCES. Family, yeah, because anyone can turn pensioners from their right to their left, but there's your mother not coping, and your father, god rest him, was fucking useless, Lizzy's twelve and supposed to be starting school up in the convent but she's no books, Lou's three and she has croup and no one's taken her to the doctor, add in a new baby who won't sleep two hours through, and all your father can think to do was sit in his 'office' and listen to *Tannhäuser* loud enough to wake you whenever you did drop off

During the preceding, FRANCES *has brought* ANNIE *another sandwich.*

ANNIE. So you came back for me?

FRANCES. If you want to put it that way, now eat that too

ANNIE *eats.*

ANNIE. I always thought it was when Lizzy's daddy died

FRANCES. Oh yeah?

ANNIE. Because she was all on her own, that you came back to care for Lizzy

FRANCES. Your grandmother was still on the go then

ANNIE. Oh yeah

FRANCES. So I wouldn't have been allowed in the door

ANNIE. No?

FRANCES. No, no love lost there

ANNIE. –

Is it bad that I like that thought?

FRANCES. That me and your grandmother hated each other?

ANNIE. No, sorry, that it was me you came back for I meant, that you like me best like Mammy likes Lizzy best

FRANCES. No

ANNIE. That's why I thought you'd tell me the truth about Daddy

ACT ONE   31

FRANCES. –

She doesn't like Lizzy best, she owes her

ANNIE. Owes her?

FRANCES (*meaning herself*). Big fucking mouth

ANNIE. Owes her for what?

FRANCES. I shouldn't say

ANNIE. Why not?

FRANCES. Annie

ANNIE. Please?

FRANCES. –

For holding a knife to her throat when she was tiny

ANNIE. What?

FRANCES. But not so tiny that she'd forget, more's the pity

ANNIE. When was this?

FRANCES. Lizzy's father had started giving one of the older girls in the convent a lift when it rained, and then he took it into his head that she needed a lift when it was sunny too, she'd only the one school shirt the poor creature, can't be sweating through it, and then he took it into his head that they were going to get married and run away together, leave your mother, and she wasn't having ANY of that, which was why when he was at the door with his bag, no word of a lie, he's at the door and he turns around and he sees her there holding Lizzy like this

FRANCES *plays all the parts in the tableau in turn – Lizzy's father at the door; Bernie holding an imaginary tiny Lizzy with one hand and an imaginary knife with the other; tiny Lizzy with the imaginary knife at her throat.*

ANNIE. Holding a knife?

FRANCES. Might even have been this one

She touches the knife in question.

ANNIE. Oh my god

FRANCES. She was never going to, mind, but to make him believe she had to make Lizzy believe

ANNIE. –

Wouldn't she?

FRANCES. Wouldn't she what?

ANNIE. Have hurt her?

FRANCES. You think she'd take a knife to her own daughter?

ANNIE. You just told me she nearly did

FRANCES. –

Well she didn't, in the end, and we'll never have to find out

ANNIE. Christ

FRANCES. Which is why I always had time for your father, because fucking eejit that he was he wasn't as bad as the other fella

ANNIE. I've never heard any of this

FRANCES. She doesn't like to talk about it

ANNIE. Lizzy or – [our mother]?

FRANCES. I wouldn't ask either of them

ANNIE. No, of course

FRANCES. And Lizzy was only two or three, she might not even remember, might be best to say nothing at all

ANNIE. Of course

FRANCES. Promise?

ANNIE. –

Is it mad to say I wish it was me? That she'd threatened, I mean

FRANCES. It's mad if it's true

ANNIE. Because then she'd go easy on me, and if I didn't even know it had happened – [then what harm?]

FRANCES. But she would, and you wouldn't like what it meant for ye [your relationship]

ANNIE. I could have gotten to go to college in Dublin

FRANCES. That's nothing to do with it

ANNIE. No?

FRANCES. That's Lizzy's money from her father, that's why she's always on about French fellas with beards

During the preceding, FRANCES *has picked up a third sandwich to bring to* ANNIE, *but in bringing it to her she bumps into the obtrusive washing machine.*

This fucking thing

ANNIE. You alright?

FRANCES. Thirty-three inches, in all the brochures, clear as day, a feature because it's So Compact, thirty-three inches exactly, but would your father measure the counters before he bought it?

ANNIE. No?

FRANCES. Would he fuck, and would she replace it when it turns out all the counters are thirty-one-and-a-half inches? Would she fuck, because then she'd have to admit she never got him to check before buying, she'd rather go without a kitchen table for fucking decades than admit we've no room for one because she made a mistake

ANNIE. You still haven't answered me

FRANCES. About what pet?

ANNIE. About whether, about my father

FRANCES. –

Right

ANNIE. Because I don't look like either of them

FRANCES. And would you want to?

ANNIE. And I don't look like any of the rest

FRANCES. No, you don't

ANNIE. –

I've more of your colouring, almost

FRANCES. –

Your father's your father, I can promise you that

ANNIE. Yeah?

FRANCES. And as for, me and your mother aren't very alike either

ANNIE. No

FRANCES. And the way you, it's the Spanish Armada

ANNIE. Which?

FRANCES. Your look, Davitt's grandfather Aeneas was the same and the combo of the dark hair and eyes with the name meant everyone was always asking him was he Iranian or Saudi or what-have-you

ANNIE. You're saying I look Spanish?

FRANCES. Because Spain was run by the Muslims, bear in mind, for hundreds of years

ANNIE. Right

FRANCES. Muslims from North Africa, I meant, Berbers and all them

ANNIE. No I know

–

Did you meet many Black people in London?

FRANCES. Weren't you telling me it's African American now?

ANNIE. Except if it's London they're not American, are they?

FRANCES. Right

ANNIE. Wouldn't be, they wouldn't be American

FRANCES. No

ANNIE. But did you?

FRANCES. The normal amount, I suppose

ANNIE. Through work?

FRANCES. In the hospital, yeah

ANNIE. You didn't have any Black friends?

FRANCES. –

One or two

ANNIE. And did they all think you looked Spanish?

FRANCES. How do you mean?

ANNIE. Or did any of them ever think you were Black too?

LOUISE *re-enters, wearing her coat.*

FRANCES. Back already?

LOUISE. I forgot about money, could you – [help me out? Give me some?]

FRANCES. You stay here with your sister

FRANCES *exits.* LOUISE *clocks* ANNIE*'s discomfort, lessened but not gone.*

LOUISE. Stomach?

ANNIE. My back and my feet more

LOUISE *rubs* ANNIE*'s back.*

Thank you

LOUISE. Helping?

ANNIE. Loads, but come here

LOUISE. Yeah?

ANNIE. Did Frances ever say anything to you about Lizzy and her dad?

LOUISE. –

Like what?

ANNIE. About him and some young one and Mammy threatening Lizzy with a knife?

LOUISE. Oh that

ANNIE. So you knew!

LOUISE. Yeah

ANNIE. How long?

LOUISE. Have I known?

ANNIE. And who told you?

> ROSE *enters, wearing her hearing aids. They are not the finest the eighties have to offer, functionally or aesthetically, and her discontent with them is obvious. They keep feeding back whenever* ROSE *speaks.*

LOUISE. How's the battery?

ROSE. The battery's fine but they won't stop doing the – [squealing noise]

ANNIE. Turn them down?

ROSE. I can't hear them if I turn them down

LOUISE. But all you can hear is the squeal if you don't, Rosie

ROSE. It's not the volume, it's they don't fit any more

LOUISE. Any word on new ones?

ROSE. She said yes, but then Daddy died and now today – [I pissed her off]

ANNIE. Well you know what you have to do

ROSE. No?

ANNIE. Let Mammy threaten you with a knife

LOUISE. Ah Annie

ANNIE. Then she'll get you whatever you want out of guilt

LOUISE. Don't listen to her, Rosie

ROSE. I don't get the joke

ANNIE. It's not a joke, Frances just told me that Mammy threatened Lizzy with a knife and that's why she got to get a degree

LOUISE. That's not, she has money from her father is why

ACT ONE   37

ANNIE. Are we getting any money from Daddy?

LOUISE. Daddy didn't have any money

ANNIE. He had his salary for managing the property

LOUISE. That he paid himself out of the rents on the property, which is Mammy's, the real money has always been hers

ANNIE. Oh

LOUISE. You should know that, doing his typing

ANNIE. Not now with – [my bump? Our father dying? Everything?]

LOUISE. Still

ANNIE. I know he raised the rents without telling her and kept the difference

LOUISE. He didn't!

ANNIE. It's all coming out now!

LOUISE. Well, maybe it shouldn't

ANNIE. Well, maybe it has to

LOUISE. –

The extra money still doesn't come to much split five ways, does it?

ANNIE. No

LOUISE. Too much to hope for

ROSE. But she didn't get her degree, did she?

LOUISE. Lizzy?

ROSE. Because that was when she had TB, wasn't it? She got sick when she was up in Dublin studying and she was so long recovering she never went back to actually get her degree, she did a teaching diploma instead a few years later

ANNIE. I thought she broke her leg

ROSE. Well Mammy told me she had TB

ANNIE. And Mammy told me she broke her leg

They look at LOUISE.

LOUISE. –

I don't remember

ANNIE. Weren't you ten or eleven then?

LOUISE. Or not clearly, anyway

ROSE. But it's not like you'd forget her wearing a cast, would you? So if you don't remember that, that's sort of – [proof I'm right]

LOUISE. Has anyone said a prayer for Daddy today?

ROSE. You did?

ANNIE. First thing this morning?

LOUISE. But since this morning, if no one else has I should – [top up the prayers?] Would you join me?

ROSE. Weren't you going to the shops?

LOUISE. Right, I'll do that and then I'll – [go myself? Do it alone?]

ANNIE. Lou, are you alright? Lou?

LOUISE *exits and crosses over with* EDELE *entering wearing a dressy-dress. It isn't black.* ANNIE *and* ROSE *look at her.*

EDELE. –

What?

ROSE. I thought you were going to the shops with Lou

EDELE. I am

ANNIE. She'll go spare (*Their mother.*)

EDELE. Let her

ROSE. She'll go spare at all of us

EDELE. And that'd be different to the way it is already, would it?

ANNIE. Can it not wait?

ACT ONE 39

EDELE. I'M going spare, I want to go for a walk, see if Peter's around and wants to listen to some records

—

What?

ROSE. You'll have to wait your turn

EDELE. My turn?

ANNIE. Because Lizzy's going for a walk with him at six

EDELE. Today?

ROSE. Yeah

EDELE. They're talking about the school today? The boys' être verbs can't wait until after Daddy's funeral, no?

ROSE. He's comforting her

EDELE (*saucily*). Comforting her?

ANNIE. Yes

EDELE. As if he'd go near her

—

Ah come ON, that's not mean that's just the facts, he's twenty-five and she's forty next week, he's a teacher and he rides his bike everywhere and he plays the flute and likes Hawkwind, and she's, what, she's a Rich Tea biscuit given life and a face like a fucking smacked arse, / really really round and really really red

ANNIE. / Edele /

EDELE. I know, I'm awful, I'm evil, I'm everything except what I should be, I've heard it all before, but tell me I'm wrong

ROSE. He proposed

EDELE. Who did?

ROSE. Peter, Peter proposed to Lizzy last week

EDELE. What?

ANNIE. They went for a walk to talk about the curriculum, or that's what he said to her, and then he proposed

EDELE. –

Why?

ROSE. Because he wants to marry her

EDELE. Why?

ANNIE. Edele

EDELE. Her money, is it?

ROSE. Don't ask if you won't listen

EDELE. And what about *no more men*, *closing the account at a loss*, all that?

ANNIE. Mammy doesn't know yet

EDELE. I'm surprised you haven't told her

ANNIE. Are you?

EDELE. You being such a lick and all

ANNIE. But you said it yourself

EDELE. Which?

ANNIE. That it's all going to be different with Daddy gone, before it was always the two of them against one of us because we could never all five of us agree on anything, but now it'll be one-on-one

–

I think that's where the speeches are coming from, the speeches and the threats, she's scared we'll realise we can gang up on her

EDELE. What about Frances?

ANNIE. Leave her out of it

EDELE. Easy enough, she'd never contradict them is what I meant

ANNIE. She'd never contradict Daddy, she contradicts Mammy all the time

EDELE. –

If Lizzy gets to be with Peter, you get to be with Joe

ANNIE. Joe dumped me

ROSE. He might change his mind?

ANNIE. If Lizzy wants to get married we should help her, is all I'm saying

ROSE. Help her how?

ANNIE. Help her stand up to Mammy I mean

ROSE. Yeah but how?

LIZZY re-enters with a plastic bag of bits – butter, margarine as an alternative maybe, bread. The sisters look at her. Since we've seen her last, she has put on make-up.

LIZZY. –

What?

ROSE. Nothing

LIZZY. What?

EDELE. Actually Lizzy?

LIZZY. Yeah?

EDELE. Where's the Sellotape?

LIZZY. –

It's in the drawer

EDELE. Thank you Lizzy

EDELE goes to the drawer for the Sellotape.

ANNIE. You look nice, Lizzy

LIZZY. Thank you – (*To* EDELE.) why are you dressed up?

EDELE. So Peter proposed to you?

LIZZY (*to* ANNIE *and* ROSE). Thank you very much [for telling her]

EDELE. Why shouldn't they tell me?

LIZZY. Because you can't be happy for anyone else

EDELE. No?

LIZZY. No, you think everything good should happen to you or it isn't good, it's a Profound Injustice, / a Perversion of the Natural Order

EDELE. Oh that's me is it?

LIZZY. Have you said congratulations yet? Did I miss that?

EDELE. Oh my god you're so like the woman herself sometimes it's SPOOKY, I talk in questions so I never have to justify myself, / keep everyone else on the back foot

LIZZY. Is it my fault you don't have a fella?

EDELE. A Fella, bless, you think I'm sad because I don't have A Fella to Hold Hands with / in the front row of the pictures?

ROSE. / Edele /

EDELE. I'd say the students are rubbing off on you only I bet they sit down the back where it's dark and all, / the first-years even

ANNIE. / Edele, STOP /

EDELE. So word to the wise, don't try to act the innocent with Peter, he doesn't like it and it / really, really, really, really, really, really REALLY doesn't suit you

LIZZY. If this is you proving you're happy for me I'd HATE to see you envious, / I really would /

EDELE. / Envious? Of what? Peter marrying you so you'll have to make him breakfast as well as give him your 'extra' sandwich every day at lunch? Which, by the way, is PATHETIC, even if it worked, ESPECIALLY because it worked in fact, I mean can you not see how it's a bit tragic that a bit of bread and cheese at regular intervals is all it took to get him to propose, like he's a fucking mouse /

During the preceding, ROSE *crosses and turns on the radio full-blast to general displeasure, overlapping with* EDELE's *Lizzy-specific displeasure.*

LIZZY. / AH ROSIE, COME ON /

ROSE. / IF YOU WON'T LISTEN TO ME, I WON'T LISTEN TO YOU /

FRANCES and BERNIE enter from opposite directions, drawn by the noise, which makes ROSE turn off the radio again, and EDELE clocks their mother too late to wind down fully. A silence.

BERNIE. –

(*To* EDELE.) Did I not tell you to give that away? (*The dress.*)

EDELE. Did you?

BERNIE sees the glass of port on the counter, walks to it, picks it up.

BERNIE. And whose is this?

FRANCES. Mine

BERNIE throws the port over EDELE, ruining her dress, but EDELE refuses to respond.

BERNIE. –

Next time I'll scald you, do you understand?

EDELE. Yes

BERNIE (*to all*). Get out

General bustle to exit.

Lizzy, stay

LIZZY stays. BERNIE takes in her made-up appearance.

Are you wearing lipstick?

LIZZY. It's lipgloss, Mammy

BERNIE opens a drawer and finds a napkin. She approaches LIZZY and holds the napkin up to her mouth.

BERNIE. Spit

–

Spit

LIZZY. I'm not a child, Mammy

BERNIE. You can spit or you can let me spit

> *A long moment,* BERNIE *moves to spit on the napkin and* LIZZY *flinches,* BERNIE *looks at her with a sense of challenge, and* LIZZY *finally, grudgingly, spits.* BERNIE *wipes her face clean for her.*

> —

> I hear Peter proposed

LIZZY. I was going to tell you after the funeral, I was, I promise

BERNIE. What's there to tell?

> —

> You didn't say yes, did you?

> —

> You are thirty-nine years old, the age I was when I was finished having children

LIZZY. I know Mammy

BERNIE. Thirty-nine when you were no beauty at twenty either

LIZZY. I know Mammy

BERNIE. So then if you're not a fool, or a child, don't act like a fool or a child

> —

> Peter is a very good friend of yours, and that's what he'll stay

> —

> And if you had ever spoken to me the way Edele speaks to you, you would have known all about it

LIZZY. I know Mammy

BERNIE. You're the eldest, twice her age, so as far as I'm concerned it's you has left her to get the way she is, don't make me do something about it

ACT ONE 45

BERNIE *exits.* LIZZY *goes to the table. She picks up a sandwich. She regards it, she opens it, she spits into it. The act can hold on her doing so methodically with a number of other sandwiches – or, for reasons of food waste, we can end as she picks up the second, her intent clear.*

ACT TWO

After the funeral. A huge pile of all the sisters' clothes arrives in the middle of the floor. These are all the clothes they are expected to give away. EDELE *is briefly the only one present. She locates the gin and pours a huge glass. She knocks back a fair glug neat. Great displeasure. After taking a moment to recover, she repeats the action. Worse this time.* FRANCES *enters with a laundry hamper in time to see her take shot number three.* EDELE *unembarrassedly puts the bottle away.*

FRANCES. Rosie can't find her hearing aids

EDELE. Why do you think I took them?

FRANCES. I don't

EDELE. Good, because I didn't

FRANCES. I just wondered if you'd seen them

EDELE. Only on her head

FRANCES. And do you have anything for the wash?

EDELE. Will I get it back, or do you mean more stuff for the pile of St Vincent?

FRANCES. Anything for the wash that wasn't on the floor of your room or in the hamper, was all I meant

EDELE. No

FRANCES. –

You had me worried, actually

EDELE. How?

FRANCES. Because, and I'm not trying to embarrass you, I got a bit of a fright when I reached in and there was something soaking wet at the bottom, thought we were done with that when you started school, bar the occasional oops, and that's a decade-and-a-half ago now so it took me right back let me tell you

ACT TWO 47

EDELE. I didn't piss myself

FRANCES. No, the grass stains made that very clear

–

If you want to keep secrets, you really need to do your own washing

EDELE. Like you wouldn't have taken the piss if I'd started doing it all of a sudden?

FRANCES. There's that

–

It was the pitch, I suppose? Seeing as he doesn't have a car, and that'd be why it made sense to spread your jumper out too, fierce muddy this time of year from all those laps the hockey team are running to keep warm

–

I'm a little disappointed in him, I thought he'd be gallant enough to offer his coat, the night of your father's funeral if no other

EDELE. Do you want something from me?

FRANCES. I want to know what you think is going to happen when he marries Lizzy?

EDELE. I don't know

FRANCES. You don't know?

EDELE. Why should I?

FRANCES. I didn't think you were cruel enough to leave her to find out

EDELE. I'm not

FRANCES. Or stupid enough to think he'd be the one to do the right thing and tell her

EDELE. Who says he has to? He's marrying her for her money, let him have her money, she's marrying him for the – (*Bad French pronunciation.*) conversation français, let her have the French conversation, if it's, you know, convenience, it should be convenient for everyone

FRANCES. She loves him

EDELE. She's not capable of love

FRANCES. Haven't you seen her with that book he gave her?

EDELE. Stop, like we don't KNOW she reads French, like we haven't HEARD about when he went to Paris and smoked a load of hash with some Algerian lads, it's bad enough that HE loves telling that story, and calling it a story is generous even

FRANCES. But you know there's a Polaroid of him inside the front cover? Taped very neatly and everything, neat as anything she keeps saying, a Polaroid and an inscription, not that I know what it says because she won't let anyone look and it's probably en français anyway, though she was telling me all about how he did it with a proper pen with a nib and isn't his penmanship only GORGEOUS

–

I like to see her feeling loved, personally, she'd to grow up fast to look after all of ye

EDELE. Don't you start

FRANCES. Alright, just Lizzy and your mother are more like business partners than mother and daughter a lot of the time

EDELE. Because the rest of us have such an easy time with her (*Bernadette*.)

FRANCES. And as far as Lizzy not being capable of love herself, well, she loves you to pieces

EDELE. Since when?

FRANCES. Since you were born

EDELE. So what happened?

FRANCES. How'd you mean?

EDELE. Where did it all go wrong?

FRANCES. The last few years have been hard, but I don't think that's what she thinks about when she thinks about you

EDELE. No?

ACT TWO 49

FRANCES. No, I think she thinks about holding you when you were just born, and about feeding you your bottle, and how you didn't sleep a night through in your own bed until well after you'd started school, / all that stuff

EDELE. Alright, you can stop now

FRANCES. No? You're saying you didn't crawl in with me or Lizzy most nights until you were eight or nine?

EDELE. Fuck off was I NINE sleeping with you

FRANCES. Maybe not nine, but are you going to try and tell me that NEVER happened?

EDELE. –

I don't really remember

FRANCES. You might not remember but she does

EDELE. You've made your point, my sister's a saint and I'm a silly bitch, what's new

FRANCES. Last thing before I let you go

EDELE. Ugh

FRANCES. I was thinking that you haven't asked me to get you any products the last while

EDELE. Products?

FRANCES. Whatever you call them, sanitary towels or the like

EDELE. –

Right

FRANCES. Probably makes sense to just have them in the bathroom for everyone, now that your father can't object, means you won't have to get them from your sisters

EDELE. Yeah

FRANCES. But I wanted to say that if there's something else going on, if you're late or, I don't know, we can talk about that

EDELE. Thanks

FRANCES. Because there's lots of reasons, lots of ways for things to go funny

EDELE. Yeah

FRANCES. And lots of things you can do about it

EDELE. I know

FRANCES. And the only thing you shouldn't do is ignore it and hope for the best

EDELE. Do you think I need you to tell me that?

FRANCES. Well, now no one can say I didn't say it to you

EDELE *exits.* FRANCES *begins to try to put order on the pile of clothes.* LOUISE *enters, needing to speak but reluctant.* FRANCES *presents her with a garment.*

Is this yours or Rosie's?

LOUISE. Show us?

–

Annie's, I think

FRANCES. Really? I don't think of her being that small

LOUISE. Well she used to be but then things changed, you might have noticed

FRANCES. –

What's wrong?

LOUISE. Annie or Rosie might ask you if Lizzy left college because she had TB or because she broke her leg

FRANCES. –

Jesus fucking Christ, your mother and her fucking TB

LOUISE. I know

FRANCES. And what did you say?

LOUISE. Leg or TB?

FRANCES. Or did you fob them off?

LOUISE. I said I had to go say a prayer for Daddy, that's what I always do, no one asks questions if you start praying, they

ACT TWO   51

run the other way in fact, but I think we're getting close to
the date on the can with that one because it was one thing
when he was around if you know what I mean?

FRANCES. No?

LOUISE. I mean I thought, it's like in school when they ask
you what you want to be, isn't it? Because you know you're
supposed to say nurse or teacher, even if you want to be,
what, a singer or a ballerina or Pippi Longstocking or just to
work in a shop, or actually I remember Jackie McGabhann
saying she wanted to be a spy and the sister telling her she'd
have to move to Russia because Ireland doesn't have spies,
which, looking back, is exactly backwards, Russia is
SENDING the spies not taking them in, but when she said
she wanted to be a spy I remember thinking oh, that sounds
fun, I want to wear lipstick and carry a revolver, but I said
I wanted to be a nurse because you were a nurse, and that
was alright because whatever it is you all say when the
grown-ups ask you all know you all want all kinds of things
that aren't nurse or teacher, and so it's alright to say nurse or
teacher because everyone knows no one means it, it's a joke
almost, until you're a few years older and you hear someone
else say it about you, oh that's Mary Louise White, she's
good at sums and she's going to go to England and train as
a nurse, and that scares you, scares me I should say, because
they don't sound like they're joking, they sound like they
mean it, and if they mean it who else means it? Was it never
a joke? Do you really have to do it now? Do I, I should say,
will everyone be really angry if I don't go? I didn't realise
I was agreeing to forever, that I would have to be a nurse all
the time, that I'd be a nurse on my twenty-first birthday and
at my father's funeral and on my wedding day, except I'm
not a nurse, or married, though I did work for my father for
pocket money for too long and then start working in the
office in the health board because no one else would have me
with my basically no skills at all, and even then only because
you put in a good word for me, meaning I'm sort of a bad
photocopy of the two of you, half of one page folded back so
you can see both but read neither, not quite a nurse and not
quite my father's companion in life but certainly closer to
him than my mother, maybe not surprising when all I've ever

done is obey the orders both of you didn't even have to give me but I was afraid you would, but what I meant to say was that ever since Edele was born I haven't been able to shake that feeling of oh god, sudden forever, the rest of our lives on the one road, don't you dare swerve, only getting worse the older we all got, no one ever going anywhere or doing anything the way we used to talk about until we realised Mammy wasn't joining in any more, that she'd just sit there gone all quiet, and then sitting there gone all quiet wasn't enough any more so she'd leave the room and we'd be left there listening to her stamp around upstairs, loud enough that we could hear it over his records so she had to be doing it on purpose, meaning the message was pretty clear, ever since I was ten and only getting stronger, the message of none of that, now or ever, how dare you want more, how is this not enough for you when we have all the money we could ever want provided we never spend it, so all in all it feels like I can't say anything about anything because something in it somewhere will be wrong and the whole thing will just, I don't know, it'll all break unless I say nothing and all of us give all of our clothes to the Vincent de Paul and wear black until we all die, probably at the same time on the one day because I've snapped and filled the teapot with bleach

FRANCES. –

You don't have to say nothing

LOUISE. I know

FRANCES. But you need to not make it harder for your sisters when they're grieving, simple as that

LOUISE. I know

FRANCES. Your father's gone

LOUISE. Jesus Christ, I know

FRANCES. I mean it's all going to have to change anyway, so you could leave

LOUISE. Leave?

FRANCES. Lizzy is getting married so she'll be around but not in the house, Annie is having her baby and I don't think she'll stay after that, Rosie needs another few years to work out what way she's headed but I think she'll go too, eventually, your mother will nail Edele to the floor if she has to to keep her from making the mistakes Edele is uniquely equipped to make in the big bad world, so if there's anyone could leave, first thing in the morning, tonight, right now, out the door with a suitcase, it's you

LOUISE. I don't have a suitcase

FRANCES. LOU

LOUISE. –

Where would I go?

FRANCES. Would you go to Russia and be a spy at last?

LOUISE. I don't think I'd do them much good

FRANCES. London?

LOUISE. I've no money of my own to speak of and no friends over there who'd spot me

FRANCES. Neither did I when I went

LOUISE. And how'd that work out for you?

–

I'm sorry

LIZZY *enters*.

LIZZY. I don't know why you would have, but did either of ye take my copy of – (*Ostentatiously good French pronunciation.*) *Fragments d'un discours amoureux*?

–

What?

FRANCES. Annie or Rosie might ask you if you left college because you had TB or because you broke your leg

LIZZY. Jesus Christ, Mammy and her TB

LOUISE. They were asking me there before the funeral

LIZZY. You wouldn't scare them off with a prayer, no?

LOUISE. I tried

LIZZY. And which is which?

LOUISE. How do you mean?

LIZZY. Who thinks TB and who thinks leg?

LOUISE. Oh, that's, I didn't – [make a note? Think to keep track? Have time?]

FRANCES. Ah Lou

LOUISE. I'm sorry

LIZZY. Try to think

LOUISE. It was Annie?

LIZZY. Which was?

LOUISE. Annie was TB and Rosie was leg

FRANCES. You sure?

LOUISE. Yeah

LIZZY. How sure?

LOUISE. I'm sure

LIZZY. –

Alright then

FRANCES. Your dirty book's over there

LIZZY. It's, thank you

LIZZY retrieves it. Doing so brings her closer to EDELE's abandoned glass of gin. She investigates it.

Is this gin?

FRANCES. I was cleaning jewellery

LIZZY. –

The book isn't, it's sensual but it's not prurient

FRANCES. I'm sure

LIZZY. And anyway, you read Jilly Cooper

ACT TWO 55

FRANCES. Now you leave Jilly alone

LIZZY. Glass houses is all

FRANCES. The worst you could pin on Jilly is she's honest, calls a spade a spade and an affair an affair and a fuck a fuck, which is more than you can say about – [most people? Fancy French lads?], just because there isn't an arse on the cover doesn't mean there are no arses involved [specifically *Lover's Discourse*]

LIZZY. Well there aren't any arses in Roland Barthes

–

So far

FRANCES. You know where you stand with Jilly Cooper

LIZZY. I'm sure, no offence intended

LIZZY flips open the book, and is struck by something about it.

FRANCES. Everything alright?

LIZZY. Yeah!

FRANCES. None of the pages stuck together?

LIZZY. Jesus Frances, I'm – [offended? Not like that?]

FRANCES. I didn't mean you, just that you've been going on about how neatly he taped his picture in but maybe it's not the tape alone, maybe he stuck it down with something else for good measure, like sealing a letter with a kiss but a bit more, you know, / passionate, and maybe in the heat of the moment there was some spillage of some binding material

LOUISE. / Oh my GOD, oh my god, oh my god /

LIZZY. / I'm leaving, I'm leaving, I'm leaving, I'm leaving /

EDELE enters in time to hear the tail-end of the preceding. The silence that follows them spotting her is marked.

EDELE. –

Everything alright?

FRANCES. Yeah! Brought all your clothes down?

EDELE. Nearly

FRANCES. You're in luck, we'll get the rest for you now so we can all have a tea break

FRANCES *and* LOUISE *exit. A wary moment between* EDELE *and* LIZZY.

LIZZY. Did you have this? (*Her book.*)

EDELE. As in, did I steal your French book that I can't read?

LIZZY. –

That came out very accusatory, I'm sorry

EDELE. I'm used to it

LIZZY. It's just the, there was a receipt keeping my page and it's fallen out

EDELE. A receipt?

LIZZY. And I need it back for, it was important

EDELE. Is it really a receipt?

–

Or is it Peter's picture?

LIZZY. I only ask because it wouldn't have just fallen out, he taped it in, beautifully neat, so someone must have been at it

EDELE. I think Rosie had it

LIZZY. Rosie?

EDELE. Rosie

LIZZY. When?

EDELE. Whenever I saw her last? I don't know

LIZZY. That, she, I fucking knew it

EDELE. Oh yeah?

LIZZY. She's mad about him

EDELE. Peter?

ACT TWO 57

LIZZY. Hangs out the window so she can watch him all the way down the road, did you know that?

EDELE. It's embarrassing

LIZZY. After our walk the other night when we were, I was trying to say goodbye and she kept just standing there until I sent her off to fetch me something, can't even remember what, but we just looked at each other and laughed, me and Peter, and then I was cross at myself for laughing, but then I was cross at her for not, I mean when's she going to get the message?

EDELE. Hopefully before the wedding

LIZZY. –

I hid her hearing aids

EDELE. No you didn't!

LIZZY. They're in the drinks cabinet behind the port

EDELE *goes over and fishes them out.*

EDELE. Vigilante justice!

LIZZY. Stop

EDELE. Which leaves one question

LIZZY. Yeah?

EDELE. If you thought that Rosie, if you KNEW it was her then why did you ask me if I took your book?

–

Did you hide something of mine too, just in case?

LIZZY. –

I threw your cigarettes away

EDELE. In the bin?

LIZZY. I took the pack out to the garden, smoked one, lobbed the rest over the fence into the trees

EDELE. Well look at you, you cheeky bitch

LIZZY. Guilty

EDELE. –

You could break them

LIZZY. What?

EDELE. The hearing aids, because she hardly wears them as it is she might not notice they're gone for a day but she'll notice if they break for good

LIZZY. Oh you're EVIL

–

Mammy would have to buy her new ones if they broke though

EDELE. See? Vengeance for you now, a favour in the long run, the worst you're looking at for that is more time in purgatory

LIZZY takes the hearing aids. She considers. She looks to EDELE, who is not wavering. LIZZY goes to the big glass of gin. She drops the hearing aids in.

They're not that waterproof are they?

LIZZY. They're definitely not that gin-proof

–

I'm sorry for the other day too

EDELE. Yeah?

LIZZY. For assuming that, I didn't give you a chance to be happy for me

EDELE. Oh

LIZZY. For me and Peter

EDELE. Right

LIZZY. And I think we both know why I did that

EDELE. –

Yeah?

LIZZY. Because I'm not stupid, I know what all this looks like, I did my intercert the year Peter was born, not that he's ever given any sign that he thinks I'm, / he's kind is what I mean

ACT TWO 59

EDELE. / Lizzy /

LIZZY. No, it's fine, whereas you and him are always laughing when you're together, he teases you the way he does the students and you tease him back and he laughs that big laugh, and he's lovely with me but he doesn't, / we aren't like that with each other

EDELE. / Lizzy, stop /

LIZZY. And you'll think I'm pathetic, but sometimes I'm envious of you

EDELE. Of me?

LIZZY. That you can make him laugh like that

EDELE. Because he thinks I'm a fucking eejit, he was in stitches the last time I tried to talk to him about a book he loaned me – (*In Peter's voice.*) It's HAY-gel, Edele, GAY-orrgg VILL-helm FREED-rick HAY-gel

LIZZY. What were you saying?

EDELE. It's spelled like Heggle

LIZZY. Heggle!

EDELE. There's two Es!

LIZZY. Heggle!

EDELE. Fuck off

LIZZY. What had he got you reading about Heggle for?

EDELE. I don't fucking know, I read the first page and the last page and that was it

LIZZY. –

Still

EDELE. Still what?

LIZZY. There's only Rosie is closer to him in age than you

EDELE. And Annie

LIZZY. Yeah but she's – [pregnant? Expecting? Enceinte?]

EDELE. Pregnant?

LIZZY. Yeah

EDELE. What's that got to do with her age?

LIZZY. I'm saying it's hard not to think sometimes

EDELE. Think what?

LIZZY. Just that, sometimes it seems like you two make more sense as a couple

EDELE. –

No we don't

LIZZY. No?

EDELE. No

LIZZY. Phew

EDELE. Why is that phew?

LIZZY. Because you could take him if you put your mind to it

EDELE. Better not piss me off so

LIZZY. Make up your mind, click your fingers, it'd happen, you're the most like Mam that way out of all of us

EDELE. That's a terrible fucking thing to say about anyone

LIZZY. It's why you get away with so much

EDELE. Hey!

–

I do, don't I

LIZZY. The terror of the family

EDELE. You're the one broke Rosie's hearing aids

LIZZY. It was your idea!

EDELE. But you did it

LIZZY. You wanted me to

EDELE. And that's a reason?

LIZZY. –

It is yeah, because yes you're disgraceful but you're as hard to say no to as she is

EDELE. You hate to credit her but it's like she was psychic, isn't it?

LIZZY. How do you mean?

EDELE. Mary Elizabeth, Mary Louise, Mary Rose, ANNETTE, EDELE

LIZZY. Oh

EDELE. Like she knew the two of us'd be the ones, couldn't have us dragging her mother's name down

LIZZY. I'm sure that wasn't why

EDELE. Do I sound upset? Am I missing out? Is being a Mary that great?

LIZZY. No

EDELE. Not like we need any more of them, with the three of ye and half the rest of the country probably

LIZZY. Or Kathleen

EDELE. Or Kathleen! Worse again

LIZZY. Or the worst of all

EDELE. Yeah?

LIZZY. Mary Kathleen

EDELE. Mary Kathleen! I'll remember that

LIZZY. The name?

EDELE. That Mam didn't hate me enough to call me Mary Kathleen

LIZZY. She doesn't hate you at all

EDELE. And I'll remember that you're funny too

LIZZY. The tone of surprise!

EDELE. Not called for, you're right, I'm sorry

–

I'm horrible to you

LIZZY. You're not

–

No more than anyone else

EDELE. I still haven't said congratulations

LIZZY. No

EDELE. Congratulations Lizzy

EDELE hugs LIZZY. LIZZY realises she is upset.

LIZZY. Hey

EDELE. Don't mind me

LIZZY. No?

EDELE. I'm just a mess right now

LIZZY. Because of Daddy?

EDELE. Because of everything

–

What are you going to do about Mammy and her *no men ever*?

LIZZY. –

Wait for her to die?

EDELE. –

C'mere, you check Rosie's room for your picture and I'll check all her – [hidey-holes? Treasure troves?] she's always leaving things in odd corners

LIZZY. You're sure you're alright?

EDELE. Yes! Go!

LIZZY goes – maybe because EDELE jokingly chivvies her out of the room. EDELE alone.

ACT TWO   63

EDELE. Fuck

—

Fuck, fuck, fuck, fuck, fuck, fuck, fuck

EDELE *fishes the hearing aids out of the gin and puts them back in the drinks cabinet. She necks some more of the gin.* ROSE *enters without seeing her and looks for the hearing aids.* EDELE *watches* ROSE *looking while* ROSE *is unaware of her.* ROSE *catches sight of her and is startled.*

I haven't seen your hearing aids, before you ask

ROSE. Someone moved them

EDELE. Well it wasn't me, alright?

EDELE *advances on* ROSE.

ROSE. What?

EDELE. Do you have it?

ROSE. Have what?

—

No

EDELE. Do you have it on you right now?

ROSE. I don't know what you're talking about

EDELE. Empty your pockets

ROSE. No

EDELE *puts a hand into a pocket of* ROSE's *and* ROSE *tries to dislodge her.* EDELE *goes for another pocket, and a rhythm develops –* EDELE *trying to frisk and* ROSE *trying not to be frisked.* ANNIE *enters to see them struggling.*

Fuck off Edele

EDELE. Do you have it?

ANNIE. What is this?

ROSE. Fuck OFF

EDELE. Give it to me and I'll fuck off

ANNIE. Leave her alone Edele

EDELE. Not until you give me the, wait, YES

> EDELE *gets a hold of the photo but can't extricate herself from* ROSE, *who is now fighting to get the photo back.* ANNIE *spies the gin glass. She tries to dash it in* EDELE's *face, but may end up dousing both combatants.*

> Jesus fucking Christ Annie that's GIN

ANNIE. Oh! Sorry

EDELE. Would people ever give over throwing alcohol in my face, it fucking STINGS

ANNIE. But I wouldn't have had to if you'd left her alone

> EDELE *displays the photo – her proof.*

EDELE. Ah, but if I did that then Lizzy would never get Peter's picture back, and she'd never find out it was Rosie tore it out of her book

ANNIE. –

> You didn't

ROSE. I didn't tear it out

ANNIE. But you did take it?

EDELE (*to* ROSE). You're pathetic

ROSE. Says you

EDELE. Yes says me

ROSE. And you're jealous

EDELE. I'm jealous? Are you TWELVE? I mean are you not mortified? Whatever about her losing her mind because he gave her the photo, but to steal it? Were you going to keep it under your pillow? The second coming of Donny Osmond, is it? / Only this time you're a grown woman in her honest-to-god twenties

ROSE. / Fuck off /

EDELE. I mean I'm mortified for you

ACT TWO 65

ANNIE. Give it to me, Edele

ANNIE makes a grab for it and EDELE dodges her.

EDELE. No no no, I'm not done

Stand-off. ANNIE makes another grab. EDELE evades again. As ANNIE turns away – too mature for this carry-on? Too pregnant? – ROSE makes a determined pursuit of EDELE, which takes them around the washing machine and ends up with EDELE standing on top of it holding the photo out of everyone else's reach.

ROSIE, look at me, I want you to hear, to hear and see, you watching? This is you

EDELE does an extremely immature impression of ROSE's immaturity – clutching the photo to her chest; kissing it.

ROSE. I hate you, I hate you, I hate you, I hate you, I hate you, I hate you

ANNIE returns to the fray with a broom, held so she can use the handle as a weapon. EDELE clocks her.

EDELE *(sarcastic)*. Oh you're SO scary

ANNIE takes a swing at EDELE's ankles which EDELE barely dodges.

Hey!

ANNIE takes another swing. If it can safely make contact, it does so. Or it might be a near enough miss that EDELE realises ANNIE means business.

Fuck OFF Annie

ANNIE. Give it back

EDELE. What is wrong with you?

In light of her ankles' vulnerability, EDELE hops down from her position on top of the washing machine. There might be a moment of cartoon farce with EDELE and ANNIE circling it – ANNIE taking swings with the broom above the machine, EDELE ducking behind it, and then EDELE is cornered. ANNIE takes the photograph back, exercising considerable force in doing so.

Ow!

A still moment. EDELE *spits in* ANNIE*'s face.* ANNIE *pushes her violently –* EDELE *might fall, or she might hit a hard surface hard. Whatever happens, it's a shock to her.*

You're a silly bitch

ANNIE. And you're a child

EDELE. Me?

ANNIE. And that's why he'll teach you funny dirty tricks all day long but will never ever love you

EDELE. I hope your baby dies

ROSE. EDELE

ANNIE. And I hope Peter and Lizzy will be very very happy, all the days of their lives, / right in front of you

EDELE *grabs the article of clothing of* ANNIE*'s that* FRANCES *had earlier, from the pile/a box.*

EDELE. Remember when this used to fit you?

EDELE *tries to tear it. She might succeed. She might go for scissors if she can't do it.*

ROSE. Stop, please, both of you, / just stop

ANNIE. Go ahead, shred it, like that's my biggest worry, do you think he thinks about you when you're not there? Are you that interesting when you are? I bet he goes quiet sometimes and you worry what he's thinking about, if he's thinking about how and he and Lizzy can talk in a way you can't and I don't mean French, if they understand each other better than you understand him or he understands you, and you're right to worry because they do, / they can and they do

EDELE. Well you'd know all about that, wouldn't you, boring people, because Joe Sugrue fucked you once and couldn't get away fast enough could he? Instead of go near you again he'll sit every night in Moloney's with Elaine Brogan and her greasy hair and her spotty face and her shiny shiny Pioneer pin drinking fizzy orange, doesn't say much for your company, does it? And that's not even all

ACT TWO 67

ANNIE. No?

ROSE. / Annie, don't – [ask? Encourage her?] /

EDELE. He's saying the two of you never even got that far, that it can't be his, that the baby is Daddy's, that our father's last earthly act between bouts with the defibrillator was to, well, you know, because Joe would rather watch the child you made together grow up a bastard, rather have everyone look at your child and think incest, poor mite, never had a chance in life, some people are worse than animals, that's what Joe chooses for his child rather than keep fucking you, you know that?

ANNIE. –

How could I not?

EDELE. –

I'm sorry Annie

–

Really Annie, I shouldn't have said that, any of that, I'm so sorry

ANNIE. Well that's it fixed so

ANNIE *moves to leave.*

EDELE. Annie

ANNIE. Please, please, please, please, PLEASE, just leave me alone

ANNIE *exits.* ROSE *and* EDELE *are left.*

ROSE. –

I was going to give the photo back

–

And I didn't take it out of the book, it just came out

–

I just wanted to look at it, that's all

–

He's stopped talking to me

EDELE. There's been a lot going on

ROSE. But he still talks to you

EDELE. That's different

ROSE. How?

EDELE. –

Doesn't matter

ROSE. I think it's the same

EDELE. Yeah?

ROSE. A few months back, he went to Dublin for that thing for teachers and came back all excited to tell me that it'll be easier for me to watch the telly soon because they're going to have writing at the bottom of the screen, because there's this group of people, of Deaf people, who are working on things like that, like this woman in St Pat's who gave a talk for all the teachers about how sign language isn't just for hopeless cases, it's not a tool, it's a language all on its own with its own grammar and everything and not just English words with your hands, and how teachers should learn it and teach it to Deaf children, and Peter was saying how he thinks that's brilliant of course because he loves languages but what did I think, he wanted to know what I thought of it all because I'm the only Deaf person he knows, and I said but I'm not even really Deaf I just can't hear very much, and that made him laugh and laugh and laugh, threw back his head and laughed at me but not mean, more like glad, you know the way

EDELE. I do

ROSE. But then the other night, when he was here with Lizzy, I said hello to him and he acted like he didn't hear me

EDELE. I saw that

ROSE. It's not fair

EDELE. I know

ROSE. –

I learned a little

ACT TWO 69

EDELE. Yeah?

ROSE. From him

> ROSE *fingerspells 'Mary Rose' – with no great confidence or fluency. Then waits expectantly.*

EDELE. –

> And what's that?

ROSE. That's me

EDELE. Right

ROSE. My name, Mary Rose

EDELE. Yeah, no, I – [got that? Understand?]

–

> All that was your name was it?

ROSE. Yeah

EDELE. Not very fast is it?

ROSE. This is just spelling

EDELE. But if it's just spelling and you know how to spell already, how is it better than just writing things down?

ROSE. There's faster ones but I haven't, faster signs that are words, but Peter doesn't know enough

EDELE. Right

ROSE. To teach me properly, he just has the alphabet on a sheet of paper, I'd need to learn from a proper teacher

EDELE. Makes sense

ROSE. Of sign language, a Deaf person probably

EDELE. If you could find one

ROSE. Yeah

–

> Do you think that all that was just butter? That he did all that just so I wouldn't mind, wouldn't say anything when he married Lizzy?

EDELE. No

ROSE. No?

EDELE. No I don't Rosie, but only because he's not very good at thinking ahead

LIZZY *enters.*

LIZZY. Have either of you seen Annie?

EDELE. Why?

LIZZY. Because I thought I saw her walking into the trees a few minutes ago, and I thought that that couldn't be right but she isn't answering when I call and I can't find her anywhere

EDELE. –

We'll help you double-check

LIZZY *and* EDELE *and* ROSE *go to look for* ANNIE. *A still moment.* BERNIE *and* FRANCES *enter from oppposite directions. A face-off.*

BERNIE. Where are they?

FRANCES. Would you ever stop telling people that people had TB?

BERNIE. When have I done that?

FRANCES. Don't waste time neither of us has, the girls don't remember TB, much less there being no treatment, much less the shame of it, they don't go all softly-softly when you say someone had it they actually ask MORE questions

BERNIE. –

And is that all?

FRANCES. I need money

BERNIE. For what?

FRANCES. Since when do you care what I use it for once you're comfy?

BERNIE. Since when is what I give you not enough?

FRANCES. Since today

BERNIE. So use your own

FRANCES. It should be you who pays

BERNIE. Why?

FRANCES. Because Annie needs to see a doctor

BERNIE. No

FRANCES. She's been bleeding

BERNIE. And?

FRANCES. And her hands and feet are swollen. She's had headaches since the wake and blurry vision since this morning, which might just be a spot of high blood pressure from living in this fucking madhouse or she might start having seizures soon

BERNIE. Can't you deal with that? Isn't that why you're here?

FRANCES. I'm only here because if I took her I wouldn't have been able to keep her

BERNIE. But seeing as you're here, make yourself useful

FRANCES. I can have her piss in a bottle but I can't run tests on it, so as far as I know it might all be nothing, but at this stage I'd worry that the bleeding might be a placental abruption and if THAT happens that's a kind of bleed you won't clean up before visitors come knocking again, or maybe at all, that's a funny shadow in the middle of the floor for all to see for the rest of forever

–

You owe it to her

BERNIE. Anything I owed I paid back, more than paid back

FRANCES. I've never denied I owe you, but we're talking about Annie

BERNIE. Because it wouldn't have been back to London if I hadn't let you stay, you'd've been lucky to get a grave

FRANCES. I know

BERNIE. Either of you, because whatever my husband might have said, whatever he might have promised you, whatever about the house in both our names for the sake of his pride, it was my decision, my decision that Annie grew up here and you got to watch, because if I'd said no he'd've had to kill me to go against me

FRANCES. I know

BERNIE. And I was the one with the nerve for killing

–

Not to mention he's dead and buried now, so the law finally says what we've all known all along, this is my house

FRANCES. –

Please

BERNIE. –

If it comes to it we'll drive her to the hospital, but she won't go to the doctor in the town

FRANCES. If she's not well and we leave it too late, if she doesn't get to a doctor in time then I'll hate you forever

BERNIE. You already hate me

FRANCES. I don't hate you, or I'd have said a few things more to the girls than I've said already, but if Annie comes to any real harm I'll say all of it and then they'll ALL hate you forever

BERNIE. If you're that sure that's how it'll turn out, why don't you go ahead?

–

Unless you're worried that they might have a few questions for you too? *Why now*, for one? Or *What took you so long? You mean you've been lying to us too all this time?*

FRANCES. Your mother died angry that I was sprung on her, would you deny it?

BERNIE. Would you deny her the right? Barely four months between us, meaning every time she looks at you she has to think he was off making you while she was carrying me, is that not supposed to hurt?

FRANCES. And did hiding the hurt make it any better? Help us do better ourselves? Are we what health looks like? Is this what you wanted out of life, for yourself, for the girls?

Because I look at us and I see terrible repetition after terrible repetition after terrible repetition, you and me, sisters forbidden to say we were sisters, and now Annie and Edele and the others, different secrets than ours but still secrets secrets secrets, and now Annie's baby, who might have hair and skin like all the other little boys and girls, god knows Joe Sugrue is pale enough, so the child might not be singled out for the worst the world has to offer in that particular way, at least, but have you heard what he's been saying? About his own child? About Annie and her father? Maybe you tell yourself they respect us in the town even if they don't like us, flatter yourself that it's humbleness and not fear means no one but Peter ever sets foot in the parlour, however perfect you have the girls keep it, but then where were they after your husband's funeral Bernadette? Why did we have to throw away all those sandwiches, why couldn't we give away glasses of a good port or a better whiskey, if they respect us so much? How could they believe Joe if they respect us? Because they do, they do believe him, so what does keeping all these secrets win us?

–

Don't act like you won't be sorry if she dies

BERNIE. But this is it

FRANCES. What?

BERNIE. We were born sorry, the two of us, you the bastard and me the bastard's sister, the whole sordid story written on our faces for anyone to read whenever we stood side by side, born paying for crimes we didn't commit, born sorry that he did what he did, and all I've ever done is try not to get any sorrier

FRANCES. And is it working?

–

EDELE *and* ROSE *enter. Anxious.*

BERNIE. What?

EDELE. Annie isn't in the house anywhere

FRANCES. Are you sure?

ROSE. We've looked, and Lizzy saw her walking into the trees a while ago

LIZZY *and* LOUISE *enter. Anxious.*

BERNIE. Have you seen Annie?

LIZZY. No, but upstairs is, did you see?

FRANCES. See what?

LOU. Our bedroom, her bedclothes, the floor even, and then in the toilet there's really just quite a lot of blood / and she said you said that was normal enough but I don't think this is normal at all, I really don't

EDELE. / Oh fuck oh fuck oh fuck /

ROSE. / Why did you have to say all that to her? /

LIZZY. / Please everybody stop shouting please /

BERNIE. QUIET, now listen, if she panicked, if she didn't take the time to tell anyone, it might be because she thought she needed to get to the doctor right away, and if she wasn't thinking clearly she might have tried to save time by walking in a straight line over land rather than along the road, / she just panicked and we'll go find her

FRANCES. She didn't panic, she was right, she thought you wouldn't help her if she asked and she was right because you wouldn't and now look, / LOOK what you've done

BERNIE. Do you want to be right, or do you want to find her in time?

FRANCES. You, you're asking me that?

ACT TWO 75

BERNIE. Lizzy will go in the car and see if she sees her along the road, the rest of us are going to go out, spread out in a line, cover the ground, start walking through the trees, and if she's there to be found we'll find her, alright?

EDELE. Alright

ROSE. Alright

LIZZY. Alright

BERNIE. Get your coats

FRANCES. And Lou, get bandages or something in case she's still bleeding

EDELE, ROSE, LIZZY *and* LOUISE *leave.* BERNIE *and* FRANCES *are left alone again. Then* FRANCES *leaves, crossing over with* ANNIE *entering – but no one sees her. She sees the audience. She looks at* BERNIE *and then speaks to us.*

ANNIE. **Traditionally ghosts are see-through**

Or, that's how you show them in pictures

The kind you draw or the kind you go see in the cinema

And that's nearly right

Because for something to be transparent there has to be nothing inside it

And ghosts are, in fact, hollow

They're not, in fact, see-through

But if you draw a ghost how they look, which is like this, they just look like everyone else

BERNIE *picks up the knife* FRANCES *used for her pantomime. She replaces it. She exits.*

Drawing ghosts transparent is, to put it how Lizzy might put it, a semiotic convention, born of convenience

And what it captures is the gap between the living and the dead

> Because when you're alive, you know things about yourself that other people don't
>
> But when you're dead, you only know what other people know about you
>
> Or, not even all of what they know about you
>
> Because they still have the private insides that you don't
>
> So you can't see what they're thinking about you
>
> You only get to hear what they say about you
>
> Which means I can't tell you much about my last half-hour of life
>
> Because I didn't get to before I died, tell anyone that is, and no one was there

LIZZY *re-enters, flustered, trying to do everything and accomplishing nothing.*

LIZZY. Keys keys keys keys keys keys keys keys keys keys keys keys keys keys keys, where the FUCK did I, unless it was, oh Christ, FRANCES? FRANCES?

LIZZY *exits.*

ANNIE. **I can tell you that Davitt in the funeral home will say Poor Thing and hold one of my hands for a long moment**

> **I can tell you he will do his best to make me look the way he thinks I should**
>
> **I can tell you that the woman I called my mother will say *her face is still carrying the weight* when Davitt shows his work, when actually she's seeing the bloat from the time I spent lying outside before anyone found me**
>
> **Maybe someone thinks *thank god it was winter, at least*, but they don't say it**
>
> **And the woman who is actually my mother will say *that make-up they've put her in would be too pale for her sisters, whatever about her, what the fuck is Davitt thinking***

And down the pub Davitt will tell anyone who'll listen that I never passed him without saying hello, not like some of my sisters

You might be thinking, how do I know if that hasn't happened yet?

It's one advantage to being a ghost

You're already where you don't belong, both outside your body and after it, breaking the rules of space, time, perspective

And if you can break the rules of time, why would you NOT be able to look forward as well as back, downstream as well as upstream, into the future as well as into the past?

That would be really silly

That would be like, it turns out it's possible to build a time machine but it can only take you to one minute before midnight on New Year's Eve of 1923 in a pub in Tubbercurry

As though the world cares that much for nuance and so little for essence

As though the world is all letter and no spirit, no pun intended

The point being, ghosts know all the things that people WILL say about them, as well as all the things already said about them, not to mention anything else said by anyone else anywhen else that the ghost cares to look into

This actually makes way more sense, think about it

You can see everything in the bright room of the world, but they can't see you standing outside in the dark

Their reflections get in the way

If you accept the reality of ghosts you have to accept them all the time

That they can always see us, here, now, whether they're looking forward or back

> LOUISE *re-enters, flustered, trying to do everything and accomplishing nothing.*

LOUISE. Cloth cloth cloth cloth cloth cloth cloth cloth, we used the last of the bandage last Easter when I sliced my hand but, is this, oh god, FRANCES? She's gone already, for fucksake

> *During the preceding she bundles a load of tea towels together, and then exits with them.*

ANNIE. **Which is why I can be here, even though I haven't actually died yet**

Which is why I can tell you that in 2004 Lou will go on a date with a Black woman

That Lou won't behave very gracefully, shocking as that may be

That she'll blurt out *you know, my sister was Black* **at a weird moment**

That her date will cope better than Lou has any right to expect and say *oh yeah?*

That Lou will say *my half-sister, I mean*

That her date, whose name is Moji short for Mojisola, will say *Yeah I guessed*

That Lizzy will never say much about me, or I'd be able to tell you what she says, but I can't ergo she doesn't

That Rosie talks about me more but I still can't tell you what she says, because she signs it, and yes I can watch her signing but no I can't understand

That the last half-hour of my life that I can't tell you about is coming up soon

That it'll take them nearly a week after that to find me

That they don't ask for help with the search, because then they'd have to tell people why they were searching

That I was always good at maths so I still am, so I know that the area of a circle increases with the square of the

radius, so that six women standing in a circle around the house create fifty more feet of scrubby forest to be searched every time they take a step away from one another, that by the time they've walked three hundred feet there's more than an acre of unsearched land between any two of them

That the trees don't seem so sparse all of a sudden when you're looking for something my size dressed in funeral black

I can tell you that when they do me find me, it's Frances who's first on the scene, because she looked harder and longer than anyone else

That she nearly doesn't recognise me because the intervening time has done its work

That she, my mother, says my name a lot, just my name, over and over

That the way she says it is a little like this: *Annie Annie Annie Annie Annie Annie Annie Annie Annie Annie Annie Annie Annie Annie Annie Annie Annie Annie*

That in [length of interval] minutes, we will resume

ACT THREE

ANNIE. **Welcome back**

It's been [length of interval] minutes for you, a little longer for us

I've been dead a day, five more before they find me

ROSE *enters at speed, carrying bed sheets heavily stained with blood. As soon as she can she puts them down – recoils from them in fact. Their feel? Their smell? She retrieves the hose for the sink-filling attachment – something is amiss. She looks closer. There is blood on the hose. She is very disturbed and cries out loudly.* LOUISE *enters.*

LOUISE. What?

ROSE. It's, there's blood here as well

LOUISE. Underneath?

ROSE. On the hose

LOUISE. Christ, did it come out of the machine?

ROSE. I haven't put the sheets in the machine yet

LOUISE. Oh

ROSE. And it's dry, but – [it's still horrible? That's not any better?]

LOUISE. So where'd it come from?

ROSE. How should I know? I hate this, I hate this so much, why is there blood everywhere? / Why is everything so horrible

LOUISE. Rose, love, I need you to calm down

ROSE. Why should I? Daddy's gone and Annie's missing and there's blood everywhere, / how are we ever supposed to act normal ever again with everything that's happened?

LOUISE. Look, do you want a little drink or something to settle your nerves? Get you through the next few days, the shock will wear off and we'll work it out

LOUISE *goes to the drinks cabinet. She removes a bottle of gin, which is all but empty.*

God, we're motoring through this

ROSE. I don't want a drink, I want to live somewhere else

ROSE *exits.* LOUISE *alone – in one sense.* ANNIE *watches her.* LOUISE *pours herself the last of the gin. Unlike* EDELE, *she uses a mixer. She sits and sips.*

ANNIE. **Joe Sugrue was very gentle when we fucked in his car**

Or, not gentle, but driven and amazed by turns

The feel of that, **he said on more than one occasion**

Or *the feel of you*

The feel of you is beautiful

Inspired if not inspiring

And I was usually moved that he was moved to say something, however obvious

I would say *thanks!*, **or** *mm-hmm!*

Or he would stop, sometimes, pushed as deep inside me as the two of us together could push him, stop suddenly to turn his head and kiss the place where my thigh became my knee

This soft flesh here

Something of a sexual Einstein, bow stopping on the strings of the violin, arrested by an equation describing the music he was just playing

Stepping out of ecstasy to see it better

He would say *I love you* **into my mouth as he came**

And he does the same with Elaine Brogan

And he calls her his first girlfriend when his daughters ask was there anyone before their mother

Which, if we're being legalistic, is not not true

Across our six months, neither of us ever called the other anything but *you*

And we never discussed the baby

He heard from someone else, and the next time I saw him he was holding hands with Elaine

I didn't confront him

I didn't want to have to hear what he'd say, what lies he'd tell

Or not any sooner than I had to

Frances was disappointed in me for making it easier for him

And she told me there were lots of things I could do about it

And was I really really really sure I wanted this

And I said yes

There must have been a reason, but I didn't tell her so I can't tell you for certain

But to speculate, maybe it was the same as with Joe?

I didn't want to have to see her face if I said no, I'm not sure I want it, let's do one of the lots of things I can do about it

In case she looked relieved

Because she didn't want to be a grandmother, any more than she had wanted to be a mother

If I said no to the baby she could have said no to me

But I didn't so she didn't

I think I had chosen a name, but I didn't tell anyone so I can't tell you

I could speculate again, but we'd be here a long time

There's a lot of children who were never named, but there's even more names

EDELE *enters. Physically unwell.* LOUISE *jumps, reflexively tries to hide that she's drinking, realises she doesn't have to.*

EDELE. Relax, do you think I care?

LOUISE. Edele, pet, what's wrong?

EDELE. What a question!

LOUISE. You look – [terrible? Sick?]

EDELE. I know

LOUISE *feels her forehead.*

LOUISE. You're on fire

EDELE. I know

LOUISE. Have you taken a paracetamol or anything?

EDELE. Loads of the fucking things, but would they work?

LOUISE. Don't let Frances hear you or she'll be on at you about your liver, that it's dangerous to take too many at the once

EDELE. That was the idea, really, banjax the whole gammy house of cards for good

LOUISE. Don't talk like that, just don't, it's not funny, not funny at all

EDELE. Do I sound like I'm joking?

LOUISE. Not when Annie's just – [disappeared? Died?]

EDELE. Don't you dare

LOUISE. I wasn't going to!

EDELE. Don't start talking as if she's dead because she's not

LOUISE. Alright

EDELE. We don't know

LOUISE. Alright

EDELE. So don't act like you know, like she, like the worst has already happened

LOUISE. I won't if you don't talk about hurting yourself

EDELE. That wasn't what I was saying

LOUISE. Then what was that supposed to mean?

EDELE. That I wanted to be sick

LOUISE. Why?

EDELE. Or even sicker, I should say, because I'm fucking pregnant, amn't I?

–

As well, I'm pregnant as well, just like Annie, so you can say it

LOUISE. Say what?

EDELE. I can see you thinking it

If it is not horribly forced, they might even laugh here.

LOUISE. –

What are we like?

EDELE. I know

LOUISE. For god's sake like

EDELE. It's ridiculous

LOUISE. And does paracetamol even, does that work?

EDELE. Clearly not, but in my own defence it's not like it was my first choice, I've drunk most of the gin over the last few days but looks like that doesn't work on the instalment plan, more of an all-or-nothing kind of thing, and I know you're supposed to take a hot bath as well but we've only the one bath between all of us, so it's been quite hard to get my sneaky gin-drinking rota to line up with the household's bathtime rota, how many ways is that? Tried poisoning it out, scalding it out, washing it out, haven't quite worked up the courage to fling myself down the stairs, partly because it's so hard to do discreetly, I know ye have no great opinion of me but I don't think anyone will believe I've forgotten how to walk

LOUISE. Washing it out?

EDELE. Yeah, didn't work

LOUISE. What do you mean?

EDELE. What do you think it means?

LOUISE. Jesus Edele

EDELE. Don't Jesus Edele me, it's supposed to work isn't it? Don't tell me you've never heard that

LOUISE. You didn't use the hose off the washing machine, did you?

EDELE. WHAT

LOUISE. Just because there was blood on it there when we went to do the sheets

EDELE. Jesus, no

LOUISE. Good

EDELE. I think that's from when, from right after

LOUISE. Right

EDELE. From when I cleaned the bathroom, my hands

LOUISE. Of course

EDELE. And why would I do that anyway?

LOUISE. Do what?

EDELE. Use a hose or, it's not like it's hard to get to

LOUISE. But for it to work, you'd need to reach – [deeper? Your womb?]

EDELE. What?

LOUISE. As in, it's not enough to mop the hallway, you'd need to clean the nursery

EDELE. –

Are we talking about the same thing?

LOUISE. If you didn't want to have the baby

EDELE. Yeah, but what are you talking about?

LOUISE. Never mind, have you hurt yourself?

EDELE. What do you mean?

LOUISE. Given yourself cuts or, if you've an infection that might be the temperature

EDELE. I don't think so

LOUISE. And does Peter know?

EDELE. –

What are we like?

LOUISE. How do you mean?

EDELE. All of us running around, thinking we're so clever, so good at keeping secrets, and actually everyone knows everything and just never says

–

I came down to wait for him to call

LOUISE. To tell him?

EDELE. Did that already and he said he needed some time to think, this is to find out

LOUISE. What he's decided to do?

EDELE. What he's been thinking, yeah

LOUISE. –

Did he say he'd marry you?

EDELE. No Louise, he did not trick me into letting him fuck me by saying he'd marry me

LOUISE. I don't think that's a stupid question

EDELE. It isn't, no

LOUISE. That happens

EDELE. It does, but in this case he tricked me into letting him fuck me by saying he'd fuck me

LOUISE. I get it, thanks

EDELE. Are you really embarrassed by that? You've never wanted that, no?

LOUISE. Honestly?

EDELE. Go on

LOUISE. I feel like I never want anything

EDELE. –

Come here

LOUISE. What?

EDELE. Frances is Annie's mother, right?

LOUISE. –

No?

EDELE. Why did I never ask you straight out? You're a terrible liar

LOUISE. I'm not

EDELE. Do you believe in God?

–

See? When you're on the spot you panic and go quiet, or you start waving the rosary beads around to scare people

LOUISE. You know I do that?

EDELE. Everyone knows you do that

LOUISE. –

I have wasted so much time saying prayers I didn't want to say

EDELE. Nice to think at least one of us will get into heaven

–

So our cousin, not our sister

LOUISE. She was our half-sister

EDELE. Is

LOUISE. Is

EDELE. But how does that work?

LOUISE. Which?

EDELE. You said she was our half-sister?

LOUISE. Yes

EDELE. –

  Oh

LOUISE. Yeah

EDELE. So Daddy and Frances

LOUISE. Yeah

EDELE. But then three years later with Mary Rose

LOUISE. Yeah

EDELE. Mammy and Daddy again

LOUISE. Yeah

EDELE. And four years later with me

LOUISE. And, and Frances never left but after Annie was born she and Daddy didn't even look at each other

EDELE. No wonder we didn't know him, he must have hated us

LOUISE. Why?

EDELE. Me and Rosie, his apology babies, 'sorry I fucked your sister' written on our faces

LOUISE. It wasn't that

EDELE. No?

LOISE. He didn't feel like he deserved you after what he did, I think

EDELE. And that was enough for Mammy? That Daddy and Frances didn't, that it was over?

LOUISE. Why don't you ask her?

EDELE. I take it back

LOUISE. Which?

EDELE. About everyone knowing everything, there's still some secrets left

LOUISE. –

Have you talked to her?

EDELE. Who? Mammy?

LOUISE. No, GOD no, Frances is who I meant, about your, about the situation

EDELE. I thought it was too soon

LOUISE. Maybe, but it's definitely too soon to do all this again

–

Not that you're going to, we won't let anything happen, and Frances will be feeling that more than anyone so you sit down, wait here, let me get her

EDELE *waits. She looks at the pile of bloody sheets. It is unbearable to do so for long, so she stuffs them into the machine, then washes her hands fervently. As she does so,* ANNIE *turns on the radio softly. It might play 'No More "I Love You"s' – the original by The Lover Speaks.* EDELE *looks at it, extremely spooked. She leaves the room in a hurry.*

ANNIE. **After a while, you get bored of seeing what people have said or will say about you**

You're dead, you're not changing, so what they're saying doesn't change that much either

A ghost's eye is caught by motion, just the same as in life

In a year or two Mary Louise will walk into the London Irish Women's Centre

And a woman will ask her *Are you here for the lesbian céilí* **with a big big smile**

And even though the answer is *yes***, a friend gave her a leaflet and she promised to look in at least, Mary Louise won't say** *yes*

She won't say anything

As it happens, this lesbian céilí is a fundraiser

Organised by a group who let Spanish and Irish women sleep on their couches, drive them to the clinic the next morning, then in the evening back to Holborn or Paddington or Heathrow where they met them in the first place

But even if you save them the cost of a hotel and a taxi, the visit to the clinic itself has to be paid for

To say nothing of plane tickets

Hence the céilí raising funds

All of which means Lou could lie and say she only cares about the cause, that the cause is the only reason she's here at this lesbian céilí, no point flirting with her

So maybe this time her silence is her friend

A phone rings in another room. After a moment, ROSE *enters, looking for someone to answer it.*

ROSE (*broadcasting*). THE PHONE'S RINGING

–

SOMEONE ANSWER THE PHONE

–

Fucksake

ROSE *leaves to answer the phone.*

ANNIE. **In 1999 Mary Rose will have an abortion in Liverpool**

The taxi driver who drives her from the clinic back to the port has a Deaf sister, so they have that conversation

The *What Do You Mean ISL and BSL are different* **conversation**

Maybe she's glad of it, because it means they don't talk about anything else

She hasn't told her boyfriend about the pregnancy

He's Deaf too

If the topic comes up he says things like *they sterilised our mothers without asking, and now we're doing it to ourselves without them having to ask*

She gets the money from Mary Louise

Or, more accurately Mary Louise tells her to meet someone in Dublin

Who turns out to be a twenty-year-old girl in a torn T-shirt who gives her some money, tells her where to ring, how long to rest for, all that

The girl's under strict instructions to look after Rosie the way Lou would like to

But to look after her she'd have to talk to her face to face

And even if that prospect were easy, going back to Ireland isn't

Whereas Mary Rose hates to leave Ireland, and she finds herself telling the girl this

And then she finds herself saying *I'm nearly forty, I never really wanted to because the women in my family have had a terrible time on the whole and I really really REALLY don't want to now*

During the preceding, FRANCES *enters. She's in ribbons. She now turns off the radio. She sits in silence.*

When Frances worked in London, there was a hospital porter she liked named Lennox

He was Guyanese, and he didn't take offence when she complimented his English

But she knew she'd said something wrong because of how he laughed

And he was kind, explaining, but she wished he hadn't had to

He had asked her to go for a walk with him right before she got the call asking her to come home and help her sister with the children

Which she could have ignored, a call from the family who never gave her anything

Except for it was her sister, who never asked her for anything either

And she had said yes, to the walk that is

But she didn't tell him she was leaving

ROSE *re-enters*.

FRANCES. Did you answer? Is there news?

ROSE. Yeah

FRANCES. Could you hear them?

ROSE. Yeah

FRANCES. And who was it?

–

Rosie?

–

Rosie can you hear me? Is there news?

–

Beginning to wave to catch her attention.

ROSE. I heard you, I can hear you

FRANCES. Is there news about Annie?

ROSE. It was Peter

FRANCES. Looking for Lizzy?

ROSE. Looking for Edele, actually

FRANCES. –

Why?

ACT THREE 93

ROSE. I don't know, because my hearing aids don't work since they got all wet, and I was calling and calling for someone else to answer the phone but no one else answered, so I had to pick up, and he said something about Edele, and I was listening carefully, I was, because I knew I'd missed something and I didn't want to miss any more, but he must have been waiting for me to answer because he said *did you get that Rosie* really loud and I said *what*, and he said *for fucksake Rosie, don't pick up the fucking phone if you can't have a normal fucking conversation*

FRANCES. –

　I'm sorry pet

ROSE. Don't call me pet

FRANCES. Sorry

ROSE. I've never been your pet

FRANCES. –

　Well then I'm sorry, Rosie, but he's made it clear what you should do, hasn't he

ROSE. How do you mean?

FRANCES. If that's how he treats you you don't want him talking to your sisters, do you?

　–

　Might be best to not even mention to Edele he called

ROSE. –

　Do you think I'm stupid?

FRANCES. Sorry?

ROSE. Because I notice things, like Edele and Peter, like you never talk to me

FRANCES. –

　I'm talking to you right now, amn't I?

ROSE. No but, back when things were normal, whenever it was all of us all together you'd just talk and talk without looking at me, and if I couldn't understand you'd never stop and go back to explain, even if I asked, so everyone else would be laughing and laughing and I'd just be sitting there feeling stupid unless Annie told me what I missed, because she always did that, and now that Annie, who really was your pet, without Annie here you just ignore me all the time unless you want something

FRANCES. –

I never meant to, Rosie, I'm sorry

ROSE. Well you did, so if you're asking me for something, if you want something, want Edele and Peter broken up, want me to say something to Edele to make that happen, I want to say the opposite

FRANCES. You could cause a lot of harm that way

ROSE. How much worse can it get?

FRANCES. Let's hope we don't find out

FRANCES *exits to look for* EDELE. *After a moment* EDELE *enters from the opposite direction.* ROSE *and* EDELE *regard each other warily.*

EDELE. Did I hear the phone?

ROSE. No

EDELE. You sure?

ROSE. Did you break my hearing aids?

EDELE. –

It was actually Lizzy

ROSE. Do you think I'm stupid?

EDELE. No, Rosie, I don't

ROSE. So why do you think I'd believe that?

EDELE. Because, and look me in the eye, it's true, I watched her do it, I watched her and I didn't stop her but I didn't break your hearing aids

ACT THREE 95

ROSE. I don't believe you

EDELE. That's fair enough

ROSE. I think it was you

EDELE. Alright then, it was me

ROSE. Why?

EDELE. Because I'm a silly bitch, I suppose, I make everything worse, I can't help it

ROSE. The phone did ring

EDELE. Was it Peter?

ROSE. Yeah

EDELE. And did he say when he'd ring back?

ROSE. He wasn't ringing for you

EDELE. –

No?

ROSE. He asked for Lizzy

EDELE. –

He didn't say anything about me?

ROSE. One thing

EDELE. Yeah?

ROSE. He said not to call him any more

EDELE. –

Right

ROSE. Ever, because he's marrying Lizzy, and I agree that that's good, that the rest of us need to just grow up, grow up and stop thinking that every boy who acts nice is nice

EDELE. –

He's really hurt you, hasn't he

ROSE. Are you really asking?

EDELE. Of course I am

ROSE. Too late

> ROSE *exits and crosses over with* LIZZY *entering.* LIZZY *catches the tension/upset.*

LIZZY. What's wrong?

—

> Edele?

EDELE. Nothing, just, let's see now, Annie's missing, Frances can't stop crying, Mammy won't admit that's what's happened, leaves the room if you say Annie's name, oh, and, I just found out you've all been lying to me my entire life

LIZZY. Oh?

EDELE. To all of us, that it's been more lies than anything else the whole way along

LIZZY. I don't know what that's supposed to mean

EDELE. Don't even try, alright? I've spoken to Louise, I've all the proof I could ever need and more, and if you stand there tying yourself in knots to deny it you're just going to end up looking even more of a fucking fool than normal

LIZZY. –

> I was not ready to be your mother

EDELE. –

> MY mother?

LIZZY. –

> What about your mother?

EDELE. You said you weren't ready to be my mother

LIZZY. I misspoke

EDELE. No you didn't

LIZZY. I did

EDELE. No you didn't

LIZZY. I did

EDELE. No you didn't, and if you say you did one more time I will smack you right in your lying mouth – what I was going to say was, I was going to say that Frances is Annie's mother and if she, if the worst, if it turns out you let her die without ever knowing I don't know how you can live with yourself, how you've lived with yourself this whole time

LIZZY. You meant Annie

EDELE. Yeah

LIZZY. Annie and Frances

EDELE. One lie amongst many, looks like

LIZZY. I never wanted to

EDELE. No?

LIZZY. To lie, but I was thirteen

EDELE. When Annie was born

LIZZY. Yes, and when Mammy, when Mammy AND Frances, when all the grown-ups all tell you it's the right thing to do / and you're that age

EDELE. To lie

LIZZY. Yes, it's so so so so hard, and even a year or two later you know better but not then you don't

EDELE. A year or two after Annie was born

LIZZY. Yes

EDELE. After Frances had Annie

LIZZY. Yes, but by then it feels too late to go back, you've already told the lie, if you start telling the truth now it can only make things worse and you're still guilty

EDELE. Christ

LIZZY. And I'm sorry that this is how this is all coming out

EDELE. No no no, it means a lot, knowing you knew better by the time you decided to lie to me

–

You're my mother

LIZZY. I had you

EDELE. When you were twenty

LIZZY. Yeah

EDELE. You never broke your leg OR had TB

LIZZY. No

EDELE. And who was my father?

LIZZY. Does it matter?

EDELE. Does it matter?

–

Was it Daddy?

LIZZY. Jesus, no

EDELE. Some good news

LIZZY. How could you think that?

EDELE. How could I not? As though we're above it? What are we above?

LIZZY. He was a boy, it was a silly small thing until it wasn't, I never thought it would go the way it went

EDELE. So why keep me? Why not get rid of me before I was ever born, live the life you'd planned? Why keep me, keep me but not claim me? Why not give me to someone, some family, who'd be proud to say I was theirs?

LIZZY. Honestly?

EDELE. Please, now or never

LIZZY. I never even thought of it, not until it was too late, Mammy found out and decided for me what we'd do, and I let her

EDELE. Jesus Christ

LIZZY. I was the age you are

EDELE. And?

ACT THREE 99

LIZZY. Would you want that choice?

EDELE. –

I've been fucking Peter

LIZZY. –

Do you think I don't know that?

LOUISE *enters, clocks the tension.*

LOUISE. Frances is coming now

EDELE. Did you know?

LOUISE. –

Know what?

LIZZY. Don't, Lou

LOUISE. Is there news about Annie?

LIZZY. She knows, Lou

EDELE. Did you know?

LOUISE. Yes

EDELE. –

I hate you

LOUISE. –

I love you

EDELE. And this is how you show it?

–

I hate that we only say that when we've hurt each other,
I hate that even when you tell me the truth it feels like you're lying to me because you're telling it for the wrong reasons,
I hate that I can't tell the difference

–

I never had a chance

LOUISE. Edele

EDELE. Here, with all of you, how was I supposed to end up a human being? I've felt like a monster so many times, but how was I supposed to be anything else?

EDELE *moves to exit, and encounters* BERNIE *entering.*

Sorry, MOTHER

EDELE *exits.*

BERNIE. What's wrong with her?

LOUISE. She's found out

BERNIE. –

Who told her?

LIZZY. No one told her, she found out

BERNIE. It was you then

LIZZY. And what if it was? Are we worse off than we were?

BERNIE. You can always be worse off

LOUISE. Is that what you tell yourself? To make it all alright? That it could always be worse, that you could always have done something worse, that we should be grateful you have only hurt us this much and not more?

BERNIE. Go on then

LOUISE. Go on what?

BERNIE. Tell me it's all my fault

LOUISE. Isn't it? You made us lie

BERNIE. That was me was it? Sewed your mouth shut? Held a gun to your head? Every moment of every day since Annie was born? It's a wonder I got anything done, one-handed, / following you around everywhere

LIZZY. Mammy there's something I want you to know

BERNIE. Well?

LIZZY. –

I spit in your food

BERNIE. Oh yeah?

LIZZY. Not every meal but I wish it had been, and it's been years, years and years

BERNIE. –

And do you want me to be angry?

LIZZY. I want you to know

BERNIE. Is that supposed to shock me? Surprise me? I've known all along you're a coward, that you hate me but can't face me, want your own way but are scared of getting it, small wonder when you think how it's turned out for you when you have gotten your way

LIZZY. I don't regret Edele

BERNIE. And that's easy to say for you, isn't it? Because it's easy for you to make it all my fault, say I made you, you never had any choice, as though not liking your choices means they aren't choices, / like a child, like an honest-to-god child

LOUISE. I hate you, I hate you, I hate you so much

BERNIE. Yeah? Tell me all about it so, do you want to kill me?

LOUISE. No

BERNIE. You sure?

LOUISE. Do you want me to want to?

BERNIE. Do you want to hurt me even?

LOUISE. It'd be a change of pace

BERNIE. Go on then, slap me in my big evil face, get me back for all the ways I've hurt you, all the lies I made you tell, slap me, punch me even, knock a tooth out, one in the front, so everyone who looks at me will know how much you hate me, I deserve it don't I?

–

Do you not want to?

LOUISE. What would I gain?

BERNIE. What would you lose? My good opinion? Do you think you have that? And it might feel great, might be just what you've needed, so why not do it?

–

Do it

–

DO IT

–

Unless you don't want to lose your moral high ground, unless you don't want to live as someone who slapped her mother, unless you like everything being my fault / and don't want to spoil it now

LIZZY. Mammy, stop talking, look at me

BERNIE. What?

    LIZZY *spits in* BERNIE's *face*.

–

Fair play, Mary Elizabeth, fair play

–

What does it feel like to make a choice?

LIZZY. I'm marrying Peter and you can't stop me

BERNIE. As if I'd have to? As if he'd have you now? With the stories about Annie flying? There isn't enough money in the world to sweeten that deal

    LOUISE *grabs her mother's necklace and pulls hard enough to snap it at the clasp. It comes away in her hand. This might hurt* BERNIE, *or it might just shock her – genuinely.*

LOUISE. –

None of us will be at your funeral, and we're going to sell everything to anyone who'll take it, and after a while it'll be like we were never here

BERNIE. What'll I care? It's not like I kept it all for you lot, I kept it all so no one could say I was the one lost it, you go right ahead and lose it all, give it all away, set it all on fire, at your leisure

ROSE *enters during the preceding. Everyone falls silent and still.*

ROSE. –

What?

BERNIE. Nothing

LOUISE. Look at you, you can't stop lying even now

BERNIE. You tell her then, you decide what to say

ROSE. Tell me what?

LOUISE. Lizzy is Edele's mother

ROSE. I know

LIZZY. –

You know?

ROSE. You said the other day you didn't finish your degree because you broke your leg, trying to be really casual, but Lou wouldn't say if she remembered you wearing a cast, Mammy told me it was TB, whatever happened it was the year Edele was born, and as well as all that I'm not fucking stupid

LIZZY (*to* LOUISE). You told me it was Rosie thought it was my leg, Rosie my leg and Annie, god love her, / thought I had TB

LOUISE. I told you I wasn't sure and it doesn't matter anyway, there are a million reasons it doesn't matter

FRANCES *enters during the preceding. Everyone falls silent and still.*

FRANCES. –

Who's seen Edele?

BERNIE. Why?

FRANCES. She's not well

ROSE. I have

LIZZY. She was just here

BERNIE. What kind of not well?

FRANCES (*to* ROSE). And?

A moment as everyone gauges everyone else's level of information. It takes too long for any pretence of casualness to be viable.

BERNIE. You cannot tell me, you can try sneak away to talk without me, but I won't rest until I know

ROSE. –

I told her Peter called

FRANCES. Jesus Rosie

BERNIE. What's wrong with Peter calling?

ROSE *looks to* LIZZY, *too late realising how revealing this is.*

LIZZY. –

You don't need to spare me, I know about Peter and Edele

ROSE. You know?

LIZZY. Edele told me

FRANCES. And what exactly did you tell Edele, Rosie?

BERNIE. What is there to know about Peter and Edele?

FRANCES. If you want us to talk like you're not here then would you ever shut the fuck up a second?

ROSE. I told her he called and said it was over, leave him alone

LOUISE. You what?

ROSE (*to* FRANCES). Which isn't what you told me to say, but that works, right?

FRANCES. Oh Jesus Rosie

ROSE. What?

LOUISE. You told our pregnant sister that Peter doesn't want anything to do with her?

LIZZY. She's what?

BERNIE. She's not

LOUISE. –

Fuck

FRANCES. You said she told you

LIZZY. That they'd, not that

–

She's pregnant?

FRANCES. / Oh god /

LOUISE. And sick, and she thinks she's on her own

FRANCES. The same thing, over and over, over and over, / over and over

BERNIE. Where is she? Find her, NOW

All but ANNIE *rush out, crossing over with* EDELE *entering. They don't see her, but* ANNIE *does. A moment of regard.*

ANNIE. **There's not much to say to each other when you're ghosts**

EDELE. **Because you both know it all already**

ANNIE. **And there's nothing you can do about any of it**

EDELE. **But there's some things you** – (*The audience.*) **might want to know**

ANNIE. **Like I died first but they find her first**

EDELE. **Like that if I didn't lock the door they would get to me in time**

ANNIE. **That Frances will be first through, into the breach, at the coal face, again**

> That she'll be saying *don't come in, don't come in, don't come in*
>
> That that's partly mercy and partly practicality

EDELE. Because I'm obstructing the doorway

> That the woman I called my mother, my grandmother, will step away from the door then, with only that much said, *don't come in*
>
> Because she knows the truth already
>
> That the woman I called my oldest sister, my mother, will insist on seeing me before she believes
>
> That the length of time before my grandmother and my great-aunt are back in this room is longer than you'd think and shorter than it felt
>
> Longer than you'd think even accounting for having cut me down, having laid me in the bed, ready to give Davitt from the funeral home a career-first surprise, two in one week from a family nothing shocking but a father and a daughter? He's never seen that before

ANNIE. Not that this is any great distinction given his field is not particularly surprise-rich, dealing as he does with the proverbial One Great Certainty, but he has already begun to talk about the strangeness of it all before he even gets the call about me

EDELE. But the point was that even accounting for cutting me down, laying me out, having cleaned as best anyone can right now, under the circumstances, just enough to render the bathroom usable though you might still want to close your eyes, even accounting for all that it's longer than you'd think before they return because of all the little reveries

ANNIE. The moments, in the midst of action, when they're startled to find they're awake and not moving

> Frances staring into the hot press, the towel she needs already in her hands

EDELE. **Bernadette staring down the road, as if looking for Davitt's car, though no one will think to call him for hours and hours yet**

You don't know where you were, just that it was not here, or you couldn't be back

ANNIE. **You don't know how long you were gone, and it's unthinkable to ask**

But the length of time before they return is nonetheless shorter than it felt

Because they both feel decades older

During the preceding, BERNIE *and* FRANCES *have entered.* LIZZY *can be heard weeping offstage at some point, then she stops or becomes inaudible.*

BERNIE. –

Well?

FRANCES. Well what?

BERNIE. Anything to say?

–

Say you told me, say you warned me, say I could have stopped this

FRANCES. –

Now we're square

BERNIE. What's that supposed to mean?

FRANCES. It means we're square, because you said it yourself, didn't you? Close the account at a loss before we've lost everything

BERNIE. And?

FRANCES. And now I've lost something and so have you, at long last

BERNIE. At long last? What have I ever done but lose?

FRANCES. All I'm saying is, you've lost a granddaughter and I've lost a daughter

BERNIE. We don't know that Annie's gone

FRANCES. You'd deny it now? Still?

BERNIE. We don't know

FRANCES. You might not but I do

BERNIE. Then stop looking for her

FRANCES. Not until I've held her, you got to hold Edele and I will hold her, I will find her and I will hold her and – [that'll fix things? Then it'll make sense?]

BERNIE. –

And to you that's square?

FRANCES. As close as we're ever going to get

BERNIE. Annie was mine too

FRANCES. NOW you claim her

BERNIE. She called me her mother

FRANCES. You really think she didn't know?

BERNIE. I'm not saying what she knew, I'm saying she called me her mother

FRANCES. You chose that

BERNIE. We chose that, the two of us, look me in the eye and tell me that isn't true

–

We chose that, and because we chose that I'm the one they'll look to for an explanation, three deaths this close together, I'm the one they'll whisper about, I'm the one they'll blame

FRANCES. Is that all any of this means to you? How it looks, not how it feels? What people say?

What could they imagine about us that would be worse than what we've lived?

BERNIE. If you think that's what moves me then you've never understood me at all

FRANCES. Then explain

BERNIE. Why should I? You're not going to hate me any less

BERNIE *picks up her knife*.

FRANCES. What's that for?

BERNIE. Scared?

–

Here's the thing about the washing machine, I would have returned it when we couldn't tuck it away only I'd made a mess of the hire purchase as well, it was going to cost us a hundred pounds more than I'd said, and I couldn't admit that I'd done the numbers wrong on the height of the counter AND the price, so I told him I'd known it would be that much the whole time and didn't care that it didn't fit his precious budget, and then I wished I hadn't because he looked so hurt, but I couldn't apologise without telling him everything so I didn't, and then because I hadn't apologised I felt like I couldn't say anything when you and he started laughing in his office, loud enough to hear over the records, however much I tried to remind you both I was there by stamping around over your heads, and because I hadn't said anything when it started I couldn't say anything when Annie came along, couldn't do anything but keep her, and because I hadn't said anything when she was born I couldn't say anything when Lizzy had Edele, all of that because I didn't ask him to measure the counters, and the funny thing is the washing machine was meant as a gift, to make things with the children easier, simpler

–

If you don't make it right right away you never can, but you never know the chance when it's in front of you, life is cruel that way

FRANCES. Is that meant to be an apology?

BERNIE. No

FRANCES. Good

BERNIE. I'm saying I don't apologise, because what use is it? You've never understood that there's no even, no quits, no square, there can't be, because the shame is the interest on the crime, the hire purchase if you like, the shadow of the prison that stretches three times taller than the prison itself, falling across your home even after you've left so that it's only the brightest of days you see the sun and even then it's glimpses, the shame climbs and climbs and climbs, grows and grows and grows, eats every moment of pride or pleasure so that nothing is truly yours alone ever again, security against your inadequate repentance, given to you only so it can be taken from you if you try to rise from your knees, you're never again sovereign, the only way to own anything, to own yourself, to hold on to anything, is to hide it all away, everything that matters, so that no one can say there she goes, the coloured bastard or the bastard's sister or or or the bastard's sister's daughter's bastard or, god, what would it even be, the coloured bastard's bastard by her sister's husband, if you want to own anything for long you have to never own up ever

–

You made the choice thinking there'd be a day we'd come clean, where everyone would know everything and it could finally be the way you'd imagined, and that's what I knew we were giving up the second we decided, that Annie would never thank us for taking so long to dig up what we buried in the first place

–

Peter proposed to the eldest, got the youngest pregnant, when she wouldn't get rid of it he panicked and took matters into his own hands

FRANCES. No he didn't

BERNIE. He did, he panicked, he couldn't see any way out, he felt his future slipping away from him so he stabbed her, over and over

FRANCES. Who'd believe that?

BERNIE. Who wouldn't, when there's evidence?

FRANCES. –

Davitt will see her neck, the mark, her eyes, and he'll know

ANNIE. **He will**

BERNIE. He'll see the wounds on her neck, and her eyes will be closed

EDELE. **He will and they will**

FRANCES. Peter will deny it and he'll be telling the truth

–

You can't be serious

BERNIE. She died pure, and no one can say otherwise

FRANCES. We can

BERNIE. But we won't

ANNIE. **Mostly they say nothing at all**

FRANCES. –

You'd do that to her? With your own hands? Your granddaughter?

BERNIE. You wouldn't? This is love, this is how we keep her, this is how she stays ours

–

They'll say she died pure

EDELE. **I died pure**

End.

ABSENT THE WRONG

Carys D. Coburn

Why '*Absent The Wrong*'?

Before we get to the wording of the title, a word on the spirit of the piece. At the beginning of *Absent The Wrong*, the character of Alice makes a video proposal for the memorial to victims of institutional abuse. There was a real competition for artists, announced in 2011; a real shortlist was selected; a real winner was selected; the monument was never built. This detail isn't offered in the play – there were many details I had to include, and this is not one of them. I was content to leave this as a loose thread in a play that thematises loose threads, non-closure, and non-closure's mirror image: serendipity. One adoptee never meets their birth parents because a nun lied. One birth mother realises her daughter lives five minutes down the road. A parrot goes missing in the early 2020s and is never seen again, but in the early eighties another parrot appears. The reunions are as improbable as the near-misses are cruel. There is a symmetry here but we shouldn't mistake it for proportion – the near-misses vastly outnumber the reunions.

I was writing *Absent The Wrong* in 2021 – before the Final Report of the Commission of Investigation into Mother and Baby Homes was published, and throughout the justifiable fallout that followed. I wanted to mark that moment. I wanted to mark the blow that it was to activists and survivors – the sense of betrayal, the confusion, the hurt.

Equally, I didn't want to simply retread the headlines. I wanted to connect that moment of disillusionment to those who had come before, to a long and spiralling history of struggle where the same fights have to be reopened, re-won, re-lost. To honour their struggle in the moment of struggle requires reckoning with what they've faced till now. (Act One of the play does this.)

Equally equally, there's a point where the duty to bear witness to the past turns back on itself. Too much documentary with not enough commentary can feel like having your nose rubbed in the worst thing that ever happened to you. *Yes, that's exactly how hard it's been – what's your point? Do you think I don't know?* You set out for affirmation and instead find despair. You have to do more than simply insist on the history; you have to insist that the history could have been otherwise – different, kinder, easier. One way of doing that as a writer is by looking for the places where things *are* otherwise, because if it can happen there why not everywhere? (Act Two of the play does this, sort of.) Another way is to imagine how things *could be* otherwise in the future, starting from the present moment. (Act Three of the play does this, sort of.)

Equally equally equally, don't utopias always feel a little insubstantial? Doesn't it always feel a little glib to be told that things are bound to get better? You have to be careful that sustaining hope doesn't tip over into damaging certainty. Adoptees, adoption rights activists, institutional survivors – they've already had too much of empty promises.

Tricky, right? You see how, in writing the play, I was pulled back and forth by two different kinds of accountability at right-angles: to affirm the power of collective action and to refuse false closure, to assert that change for the better is possible but to deny that it is inevitable. This tension is what gives the play its shape and central question: What is, what could be instead, and how? (And when?)

That question could lead you to a very traditional structure in three acts: here's where we were, here's where we are, and here's what we should do next. *Absent The Wrong*, looked at one way, is this kind of play. Act One is a fractured timeline that takes us through the last seventy years; Act Two is a farce for serious purposes in the present; Act Three is not straightforwardly in the future – remember my ambivalence about utopias. Instead we go backwards and forwards at once, and try to imagine all the futures that fan out from a fixed point decades ago. So you could annotate the three acts of the play as follows:

Past   Present   Future(ish)

It's an accurate description of the play – but it would be a shit title. A first-pass improvement: in talking about how to stage the play we talked about what the primary gesture of each act was. What *specific* act is Act One? Two? Three? This was richer. And what we settled on was this:

Searching　　　Coping　　　Hoping

Act One searches, stutters, restarts, jumps. Act Two bears up under a great weight – it's about how we live with the past in the present. Act Three dares to hope, refuses to despair, to accept the given as the necessary. *Searching Coping Hoping* is a lot stronger than *Past Present Future(ish)*, even if it's not actually good. It's still falling on the side of inertly descriptive, missing the touch of poetry or mystery that draws you into the work, that drives you to try and answer the question at its heart for yourself.

We started with times, and then we added motion through them; we could get some poetry by adding some dimension, some space, some quality, some rhythm, to that motion – like this:

A Chain　　　A Net　　　A Knot

Act One is all scenes about people who've been unjustly denied something. Lots of them are fighting lonely battles against the same big system. Their separateness is what unites them. They're discrete loops that come together to make a continuous line. They're a chain. It's strong, but it's heavy and cold. It speaks more of need than of love.

Act Two is about a community who drive each other nuts but, at the end of the day, have each other's backs. (More or less.) Lives interweave to make a fabric – the fabric that makes a bag that lightens your load, or a tie to hold fast what you can't afford to lose, or an overlayer that cuts the chill of a harsh world. Community as the source of warmth, strength, depth – where need and love come together.

Act Three centres on a small small moment. Arguably it's a moment of love. Sexual? Romantic? Platonic? You can argue for each, just like you can argue that it's gratuitous – that this is a love that doesn't go anywhere. It doesn't get to. It isn't allowed. Is it unimportant? Again, you could argue that. But I wouldn't. The way I like to think of it is that this act might not lead to anything in any clear-cut way, but it shadows everything else in the play. Or maybe not shadows – illuminates. It's a knot. A knot on its own is nothing much. A knot in the wrong place is the reason your hair won't lie flat or one of your shoelaces is shorter than the other. But knots in the right place make your net a net, make your chain a chain. Everything good in this play depends on this purposeful tangling, this noun-verb of a place where two things blurrily start to act like one.

Finally, some poetry. Some mystery too – maybe too much. Would you think a show called *A Chain A Net A Knot* was about adoptees, or would you think it was about the fishing industry?

If you've read the epigraphs for this play already, you know where the title comes from. Catherine Gallagher's *Telling It Like It Wasn't* is a history of alternative histories. Great title for a great premise. And her summary of the tort law cases in the early days of the civil rights movement is so rich: the *copiousness of wrongs* as a *special conceptual problem* posed to any tit-for-tat conception of justice. Maybe it's self-regarding of me, as an artist, to like the emphasis she gives to the creative aspect of law; if it is *difficult to imagine the conditions under which the plaintiff would exist absent the wrong*, then justice demands we get good at imagining. All the same. These words, to me, unite precision with poetry. They say something about the necessity of rage and the inadequacy of regret. They accept that true restitution for a sufficiently great loss is itself a loss; the world itself would change so much – and everyone with it – that we'd lose our current selves. It doesn't seem fair, does it? That the burden of change falls most on these who've already borne the most, who least deserve to bear more. Isn't that drama, though? Cruel irony. Intent and action not lining up neatly, cleaving and cleaving. Thus, *Absent The Wrong*.

The last thing to say is this: I feel so lucky to have made this show with everyone. Above all, I am glad to have spent the autumn of a hard hard year in the same room with my mother and my sister as we worked on it. We're blood, but I choose to have them at the centre of my life too. As the many many many people who love them without blood ties would agree: how could I not?

Carys D. Coburn,
September 2025

Absent The Wrong was first produced by Once Off Productions, and performed on the Peacock Stage, Abbey Theatre, as part of Dublin Fringe Festival on 13 September 2022 (previews from 10 September). The cast was as follows:

Jolly Abraham
Curtis-Less Ashqar
Sheik Bah
Noelle Brown
Caoimhe Coburn Gray
Kwaku Fortune
Colleen Keogh
Sophie Lenglinger
Leah Minto
Emmanuel Okoye
and Peanut the cockatiel

Director	Veronica Coburn
Set Designer	Molly O'Cathain
Costume Designer	Pai Rathaya
Lighting Designer	Suzie Cummins
Composition and Sound Designer	Jenny O'Malley
Directing Associate	Claire O'Reilly
Movement	Olwyn Lyons
Dramaturg	Kirsty Housley
Hair	Leonard Daly
Producer	Cally Shine
Producer	Sara Cregan
Producer	Maura O'Keeffe
Production Manager	Rob Furey
Stage Manager	Miriam Duffy
Assistant Stage Manager	Meabh Crowe
Costume Supervisor	Siobhra O'Reardon
Directing Intern	Maureen Penrose
Set Design Assistant	Angéle Bernigole

Acknowledgements

Thanks to Trish, Andrew, Lorraine and Grace and the IamIrish team, to Claire McGettrick born Lorraine Hughes. Thank you to Conrad from AMRI, to Caelainn Hogan, to Conall O'Fatharta.

C.D.C.

'Had Pyrrhus not fallen by a beldam's hand in Argos or Julius Caesar not been knifed to death. They are not to be thought away. Time has branded them and fettered they are lodged in the room of the infinite possibilities they have ousted. But can those have been possible seeing that they never were? Or was that only possible which came to pass?'

James Joyce, Ulysses

'As the Bakke case also illustrated, though, the difficulty of specifying wrongdoers was compounded by the difficulty of exactly delimiting the wrongs... In the case of African Americans, the copiousness of wrongs was a special conceptual problem that not only turned "history" into the culprit but also made it difficult to imagine the historical conditions under which the plaintiff would exist absent the wrong... The problem, therefore, was not that one couldn't point to past wrongs, but that in the relations between black and white in America, one could point to very little else.'

Catherine Gallagher, Telling It Like It Wasn't:
The Counterfactual Imagination in History and Fiction,

Characters

ALICE, *one part across Acts One, Two, Three. First played by Leah Minto, first written with/for Ayoola Smart. Alice has been raised believing she's Nigerian Irish but isn't. The actor playing her may identify as Black or not, but should have some African heritage.*

NANCY, *one part across Acts One, Two, Three. First written with/for Noelle Brown and first played by Noelle Brown. Nancy is a white Irish woman, of an age to be Alice's mother.*

MICHAEL / KING / MAN, *same character in Acts One and Three, different in Act Two. First played by Sheik Bah, first written with/for Ryan Cobina Lincoln. Michael/Man is Black. He doesn't know his parentage, but assumes his mother was Irish and white. King is an Irish citizen from a Ghanaian family.*

T / THOMAS, *different parts in Acts One and Two, lines as assigned in Three. First played by Curtis-Lee Ashqar, first written with/for Trevor Kaneswaran. Thomas is a Palestinian Irish man from the North, and he's a father.*

C / CIARA, *different parts in Acts One and Two, lines as assigned in Three. First played by Caoimhe Coburn Gray, first written with/for Caoimhe Coburn Gray. Ciara is a white or white-passing Irish woman with fluent ISL.*

F / FUNMI, *different parts in Acts One and Two, lines as assigned in Three. First played by Jolly Abraham, written with/for Felicia Olusanya. Funmi is the older sister (or half-sister, they don't fuss those things) of Edward. Funmi grew up in Nigeria, but Edward might not have.*

A / ANNA, *different parts in Acts One and Two, lines as assigned in Three. First played by Sophie Lamiokor Lenglinger, first written with/for Ashling Edward O'Shea. Anna has an English accent, but grew up in Kampala – she can be played by a Desi performer or a Black performer. Either way, there is something about how she relates to her life/heritage that makes Alice want to throw things.*

J / JILL, *different parts in Acts One and Two, lines as assigned in Three. First played by Colleen Keogh, first written with/for Jade Jordan. Jill is a Black woman, not necessarily but probably Irish. (In our production she was Scottish, and that was perfect.)*

E / EDWARD, *different parts in Acts One and Two, lines as assigned in Three. First written with/for Emmanuel Okoye and first played by Emmanuel Okoye. See Funmi above for background details on Edward. Additionally, it is vital that Edward really enjoys being gay.*

K / RICHIE, *different parts in Acts One and Two, lines as assigned in Three. First written with/for Kwaku Fortune and first played by Kwaku Fortune. Richie is a Ghanaian Irish man who grew up in Ireland but isn't a citizen.*

Additionally, *Absent The Wrong* features a live cockatiel. The character of Phil (as-in-Lynott) the cockatiel was first played by Peanut the cockatiel.

Note on Text

/ indicates a point of overlap. A line / enclosed / means the lines either side of it run continuous.

[ ] indicates an option for an unspoken end of an unfinished sentence.

Note on Play

Absent The Wrong can be performed by ten performers, because it was developed with ten performer-collaborators. It can be performed with a lot more people, but not fewer. The doublings/breakdown given here are as they were for the 2022 Dublin Fringe Festival premiere. If anyone is confused as to why the Act One initialled roles and the Act Two named roles have the same initial in all but one case – that's because Kwaku wanted to do more of the Ghana material in Act One, so I moved some of the doublings around from the initial schema to make that easier. Testimonial from contributors is given in italics after the heading/title, with line breaking to indicate approximate rhythms/timings. Brackets are used to show the inferred/intended completion of speech sounds that don't become full words. In our production, these were lip-synced.

ACT ONE – VOICES

There is no action in this act. We hear voices and we see faces. If the show is in a theatre with a proscenium arch, the entirety may take place in front of the curtain. Though we jump through time and space, please don't treat the transition from one scene to another as cuts. Once someone is onstage, they're onstage. No one ever pretends not to be present when they are, no one stops existing just because they're not talking. If it helps, try thinking of it as a parade. It's not that the float disappears as it passes you – you can still look at it if you want, but it's more interesting to look at what's coming next. As we begin, ALICE *is the only person onstage. Throughout,* ALICE, NANCY *and* MICHAEL *are the only people who stay themselves. Everyone else is a one-off character; once their scene is over, they don't come back.*

Two Thousand and Twelve

ALICE. My name is Alice Olanrewaju, it is the year of someone's lord 2012, and this is my video proposal for the monument to victims of abuse while in residential care

You haven't answered my email asking if you accept video proposals, but I'm doing one anyway because you should

It'd save you a lot of time, visual artists hate writing, me included

Plus selfishly, this is already tricky enough for me

Because I don't know if this history is my history or not

I was born in a mother and baby home, adopted into a white family, and I've been told by the religious order that ran that so-called home that they have No Information Whatsoever on my birth mother and father

I don't believe them, but that's not the point right now

The point is, my mother might have been a middle-class girl who fell for a Nigerian medical student in the hospital where she worked as a nurse

There was enough of that

Maybe their eyes met over a bedpan?

Or he might have been a law student, and she might have taken dictation and liked his accent

Lots of that too

And she might have asked a friend for help, who gave her a number for the helpful people who would make The Problem go away without her family ever knowing

Or her father sent her to them

Or her mother

Or her married sister who was hoping to adopt me, but then they sent me somewhere they couldn't find me

She might have died having me

She might still be alive

She might be watching me speak these words

Or my father might have been English, with a Liverpool accent, maybe an Irish grandparent of his own

Or an American, hanging around eighties Ireland even though there was no pasta, maybe a Moloney or O'Hara by way of Jamaica who preferred to explore his heritage here, knowing there's no fairytales to be found in Kingston and hoping Dublin or Cork might be different

Naively, needless to say

Or my mother might have been Black herself

She might have been born in a so-called home just like me, been sent to a so-called reformatory when just old enough, where she might have 'fallen' pregnant while still not really old enough

In which case the story of institutional abuse told by the Ryan Report is my story

But I don't know for sure

There's an infinite number of things that could have happened, and knowing they're infinite I still can't help but try to hold them all in my mind, to pass over them one by one like rosary beads, to keep them that close, to warm them in my hands, as though the warmth enlivens them, preserves them, makes them more real

As though just by thinking enough I can make the truth appear

We love alternate histories, what if Nazi Britain, what if Confederate States, what if Colonised Europe, a changed past leading to an other now

And isn't it funny how the other now always reconciles us to the now we have?

As though we don't dare hope for more

As though we're too scared to even think about grieving what might have been

Scared to realise our loss is so great that our grieving might never get to end

Which brings me back to memorials

Maybe I should say right now, my idea for the actual memorial is very simple!

It's, the Irish state should build exactly one nice house somewhere central, walking distance from somewhere you can do The Big Shop, and give it to a single mother on the housing list in that place to live in, free of charge, rent or mortgage or utilities even, until such time as both her and her kids are happy to leave, then do it all over again with another mother and her children, world without end

There's your memorial

Exactly one non-nuclear family, cared for modestly but adequately

Such a little thing to ask for, except it's never been done

Not by twenty Fianna Fáil governments, not by seven Fine Gael governments, not by any of those religious orders still pretending not to know what they know about all those adoptees, me included

That's my idea, and I started with my family so you'd know I wasn't joking

So you know this is important to me

Some more important facts:

The Ryan Report allocated five hundred thousand euro for a memorial to victims of abuse while in residential care

And let's be conservative, let's be optimistic, and let's say that the fifteen thousand survivors who have sought financial redress are most of the living, let's imagine it's 'only' twenty thousand total

That's counting only those still alive, which in context makes sense

But notice we have agreed that it is sensible, that it is rational to not count the dead, the murdered, the buried without funerals, without coffins, without names, the ones who felt they couldn't take any more any more, the reckless who met accidents teeth-first because they learned early pain was inevitable so don't fight too long or too hard because then they just hurt you more, the lifelong sick too scared to go to hospital because an overnight ward is too much like sharing that childhood dormitory again, the one with no door that you could lock against someone for your safety, your privacy, your secrecy, though the reverse sadly does not hold so that you learn, early and well, that keys are weapons

When we agree not to count the dead we have agreed not to tally, not to reckon, not to know what we have lost

We have agreed to excuse their extinction, to lose our loss itself all over again

We have agreed that the primary crime is leaving evidence, not the murders

But taking the five hundred thousand euro budgeted for this memorial I am proposing and dividing by twenty thousand we get twenty-five thousand euro per survivor

So if there's something insulting about me suggesting
a house as the memorial, maybe it's not my suggestion

Maybe it's that the budget for this memorial only buys one
house, in this the year of someone's lord 2012

It's a very small gravestone for a very big grave, but
remember: we are not counting the dead

So while it's definitely not proportionate, how would we
even know if it was?

And maybe the whole idea of proportion between crime and
correction is not just misguided but obscene

Because lives, unlike euros, are not fungible, not identical,
do not swap or cancel

Because when a debt plus interest is repaid it's like it never
existed, but a survivor paid compensation does not become
the person they would have been if they hadn't been taken
from their family, starved, beaten, burned, left lying on damp
sheets while their lungs filled with fluid and clogged, left
sitting on a potty until they prolapsed, told their parents were
dead but there was no funeral to go to or not for you anyway,
raped, sent out into the world Deaf but not taught to sign, not
taught to lip-read, not taught to read, to write, to boil an egg

They do not suddenly live in a world where there was no
harm, no so-called school, no very real loss

So what equivalence can there be between the one obscenity
called history that happened and the infinite number of
things that were never allowed happen, the infinite number
of people we could have been absent the wrong done to us
but, crucially, we never got the chance to choose to be?

Marked change in tone.

Is this too strong?

Institutions

The numbers of adoptions went up right through the fifties and into the sixties

>*and then kept going into the seventies and then once single p(arents)*
>
>*single mother payments came in*
>
>>*th(ey)*
>>
>>>*started to drop sharply*

And what would have happened in the 1940s and nineteen

>>*and early 1950s*
>
>*is a lot of children would have been fostered*
>
>>*through the adoption agencies*
>
>*but then ended up in the industrial schools*

And what happened as (*) t(ime)

>*what happened as time went on*

>*instead of p(eople)*
>
>>*people would have went to the agencies*
>
>*and an arrangement for an adoption would have been made quite quickly*

Whereas

>>*lots of the people who ended up born to single mothers*
>>
>>>*in the industrial schools*
>
>*would have been with a foster mother*
>
>>>*arranged through one of the adoption agencies*

And then when they got

>>*sometimes when they got to school age*
>>
>>>*they would have then went into an industrial school*

Two Thousand and Three

T. What I would advise, Nancy, is, the tricky thing in these cases is the relationship between plausibility and precedent

NANCY. What does that mean?

T. Well, precedent is when something has happened before / and is a matter of record –

NANCY. No I know what the words mean, all of them, what I mean is say what you mean straight-up

T. Right, well, straight-up, most of the claims you're making about your time in St Finbarr's are not, they're under-evidenced, so our best option might be to stick to those claims corroborated by other survivors' testimony

NANCY. So only say the stuff other people are saying

T. If you want to put it that way

NANCY. But isn't the point of all this –

T. No, actually, because this is the redress process, not the Laffoy Commission, what this is is, this is about guaranteeing yourself some long-overdue comfort for the years ahead, and I don't think chasing this photo thing will get us that

NANCY. But that's the thing I'm angry about

T. I didn't want to say this, but the photos, you have two incidents and one of them is prima facie invalid because it's beyond the remit

NANCY. What does that mean?

T. Prima facie?

NANCY. Why is it invalid?

T. Because you allege that inappropriate photos were taken of you on two separate occasions, one when you were a minor in a residential care institution, okay, we can bring that to them, they'll say *is there any proof* and we can have that fight, but the other occasion was, you allege, when you were an adult in a mother and baby home, just after you'd given birth, which is awful but is not what this process is meant to address

NANCY. I don't allege, it happened

T. Of course, I'm just saying what they're going to

NANCY. No I know, you're saying what they'll be saying and I'm saying what I'll be saying

T. I agree with you, I just want you to get the settlement you deserve

NANCY. And is that all?

T. The only objection?

NANCY. Or will there be more?

T. Bluntly, it sounds very extreme

NANCY. More extreme than everything else?

T. The violence, people can tell themselves it's a, a what, a momentary loss of control, / which I KNOW is offensive

NANCY. / Momentary loss of control every day, was it? /

T. But photography feels calculated in a way people will resist, someone taking your photo while you're pregnant, / and as I have already said we Do. Not. Have. The. Photos.

NANCY. / While I was giving birth, not just while I was pregnant /

T. While you were giving birth, yes. But I think the physical abuse you suffered will carry it for us

NANCY. Leave the rest out, only say what everyone else is saying?

T. Yes, it's ugly but that's the way of it

NANCY. So what about the dead? What about all the stuff they went through?

T. I'll just go get a Ouija board will I?

NANCY. –

You phoned me, I didn't want to do any of this, dig up any of this, then you ring me say Your Case Would Help Other Cases, like I'm letting other people who went through the schools down if I don't, / can I be your representation

T. / But this is the process, Nancy /

NANCY. Did you or did you not ring me asking to be my solicitor?

T. I did

NANCY. And why did you do that?

T. This is really important

NANCY. Who for?

Closing Ranks

I think coming into the late nineties early two thousands they were starting

> *to get wise and shut up(s) shop*

because bear in mind state apology 1999

> *vaccines broke in '96*

vaccine trials '96 '97

> *em*

> *that started to come out*

>> *so they're starting to*

you know they're

> *they're closing ranks*

Mormons One (Ninety-Five)

J. Have you tried the Mormons?

F. Why?

J. Up in Glasnevin, they've moved from Eccles Street, bought a big place

F. But why would they have anything?

J. It's not just knocking on doors, they go in the archives, the young ones, photocopy parish records, birth certs

F. Of people who were Mormons?

J. No, parish records

F. Oh yeah

J. But they want to help, people say, they're very helpful

F. Why?

J. Are they helpful?

F. Or do they do it, more

J. Haven't a fucking clue

Litany One

C. 1955

T. April 3rd

C. Maryann Robinson, twenty-eight

T. Patrick Kelly

C. Sligo

T. Kate Quirke, thirty

C. James Rooney

T. St Patrick's Home

C. Mary Fowler, twenty

T. Christina Mitten

C. Holles Street

T. Margaret Moyers, forty

C. George Kidd

T. Connolly

C. Jane Dalton, eighteen

T. Mary Dalton

C. The names match!

T. Yeah

C. Doesn't that mean – ?

T. She wasn't married, no, but I'm not a girl

C. Oh

T. Yeah

Odds (Twenty Nineteen)

E. What I say is, every case is different

A. But I'm asking you your, how do you see it

E: Overall?

A. Overall

E. Well, what I say is it's hard to say because society's gotten better but the law has gotten worse

A. Okay

E. As in, sometimes you'd ask a religious order or the adoption board and they'd just give it to you, or you might get told there was nothing and that just meant they didn't want to give it to you, whereas now that there's more laws saying yes, you should be able to know what info people hold if it concerns you, there's more of a waiting list too to get dealt with, so people are sometimes waiting two three years to get a birth cert with everything redacted, even stuff they know already, you say you know your mother was a Halpin and they still redact it, and back when there were more Nos there were at least more ways of finding out, too, but they've all been shutting down since they started worrying about getting sued, maternity hospitals used to give you address and age and previous pregnancies which was handy for narrowing down which of nineteen Kathleen O'Connors you were looking for, then the Rotunda fought that all the way to the Supreme Court because it's not Personal info it's Confidential Medical info, Department of Welfare used to have a letter-forwarding service that meant you could send a letter to anyone if you had a name and a date of birth, but from 2013 on you weren't allowed say you were a social worker so people stopped replying because they thought it was a scam, and now that's totally dead because of GDPR, so at this point there's nothing but the General Records Office if you're after a birth certificate, reading through every single birth, nothing but the electoral register if you have a name and an address for a parent, reading through every single voter, nothing but the telephone book if all you have is a name, and people don't really put their numbers in the phone book as much any more

A. So I should have looked sooner, is what you're saying

E. Whenever you want to know is the right time to look

A. But I could have walked into the office in the early nineties, ninety-four say, and walked out with everything I wanted to know if I was lucky

E. If

A. Yeah, big if

PCOS (Twenty Ten)

C. Is that, how do you spell that or is it – ?

K. Polycystic Ovary Syndrome

C. It's an acronym, okay

K But what it means is, it means all sorts of things, high testosterone, harder to have children, most important is there's an increased risk of heart attack and stroke

C. Wow, okay

K. So you shouldn't smoke or, the big one the big risk is the pill

C. Okay

K. The contraceptive pill

C. Yeah

K. But that's alright, isn't it?

C. For me?

K. Because you said, didn't you, that you're –

C. Gay?

K. That, yeah

C. They actually put me on it when I was younger

K. When you, before?

C. For pain, really bad period pain

K. Right, that'd be it

C. Which?

K. The PCOS

C. Better late than never, I suppose

K. You didn't know at all?

C. How would I?

K. Because she wrote a letter

C. To me?

K. That she left with the agency, a letter and a photo if you came looking, and told them as well so they could pass it on if you were adopted

C. First I'm hearing about it

K. –

You don't smoke as well do you?

General Records Office

Y y you used to have to

>*eh*

>>*sign in*

>>>*go upstairs*

I think it's called the records room?

>>*Or the research room?*

>>>*Records room*
>>>*maybe*

(n) I think they allow ten people in at a time

>>*and then*

You would find the big red

>*You'd take out your big red book*

>>>*for 1965*

(Breath.)

And

>*Then when you find the entry*

>>>*it was kind of an abbreviated (o/ne)*

>>>>*version*

ACT ONE   139

So there might be

>*five books for January*
>
>>*you (kn/ow)*
>>
>>>*I I I (d/on't)*

I'm not sure exactly of how many

>>*births there are in Ireland
>>per year*

It's a process of elimination

Eh you

>*break it down*
>
>>*to*
>
>*the births of the same sex as yourself*

that were born to

>*a*
>
>>*single woman*

So there might be a page with twenty births but

>*one or two of them*
>
>>*could be*
>>
>>>*your mother*

So

  (*Breath.*)

>*definitely an exercise*

Litany Two

F. May 9th 1970

T. Maggie Dungan, thirty-four

F. Pádraig Bissett

T. Mallow General

F. Lucinda Ellis, sixteen

T. Liam Dunne

F. Our Lady of Lourdes

T. Mary Sweetman, twenty-one

F. Jane Carroll

T. Rotunda

F. Anne Hoare, twenty-five

T. Thomas Gough

F. Rotunda

T. Lillian Scully, thirty

F. Dolores Duff

T. Rotunda

F. Georgina Lee, fifteen

T. Shelagh Lee

F. St Patrick's Home

Prayers (Eighty-Eight)

J. Whenever I prayed I always said a prayer for you

A. That's, I know you're being sweet but that's not comforting

J. Well it's true

A. But I'm the one who looked, who had to go looking for you

J. But they told us not to

A. Who?

J. In the office, we went in, they said you were settling in with your new family and did we want to go upsetting everything

A. But I wasn't

J. You weren't happy?

A. No I was never adopted even

—

J. Oh

A. Yeah

Vacuum

I i in the

   legislative vacuum you saw

      increasingly over the years

         like you would see them just

   clamping down and clamping down and

   there was no

Like th there

   there were no guidelines like until

2007 I think were the first
information-tracing guidelines but

Like I don't know if they were ever officially adopted they were

they were

put together by the

the adoption board as it was then

But again like they were quite

restrictive

too you know

At one point the adoption board were getting people to sign affidavits

that they wouldn't contact their

eh

mothers if they released em

birth certs to them

Michael (Ninety-Nine)

C. Because the first thing is, there's a lot of records and a lot of people Michael

MICHAEL. Okay

C. It's not one box Michael, it's not I can close my eyes and put my finger on it

MICHAEL. I know

C. Or even an alphabetised, it's years and years and different systems, it's not organised Michael

MICHAEL. Okay

ACT ONE 143

C. So I need you to understand that I might go and look, and it might turn out we don't know her name

MICHAEL. Okay

C. But even if I go, if something turns up, what I really need you to be clear on is, her life kept going after that

MICHAEL. Yes

C. After all that with, can you understand that Michael

MICHAEL. Yes

C. So I'm telling you I'll do my best but it can be very painful, stories of severe trauma, you'd call it, where a girl might have been forced or if the father is a family member

MICHAEL. I know

C. Her father even, the father is her father

MICHAEL. If you tell me that that's the case here, / then of course

C. I'm only saying that it can be painful, to have all this history dragged up, landing on the doorstep

MICHAEL. But I'm –

C. What's that?

MICHAEL. Sorry?

C. The line went bad there

MICHAEL. I was saying, I've said to ye over and over I have no plans to contact them

C. Well, Michael, you're a clever man, I'm sure you see that that's worse almost

MICHAEL. Is it?

C. To go through all that, to force her and her husband, if she has a husband, children too, having to think that way about a mother, and it's just idle curiosity?

MICHAEL. My da, my da who adopted me just died of Alzheimer's there, and that leaves you, you can't help but be wondering, and one thing I'm wondering is, is it not allowed for you to tell me her name even?

C. Well, people have a right to privacy, Michael

MICHAEL. I know

C. A constitutional right

MICHAEL. Right

C. But what I could do is, if you let me know what you're most eager to know then I could see if anyone else in the family was able to fill in the picture for you, how does that sound, so you can go away happy and she doesn't have anyone disturbing her

MICHAEL. Sorry?

C. Can you hear me?

MICHAEL. No I can hear you

C. Right

MICHAEL. You said you could ask the family

C. I said I could try

MICHAEL. But does that mean that you do know, that you do have records and you do know who she is?

–

Did I misunderstand you when you said you didn't know if you have her name on record?

–

Do you have her name?

Litany Three

F. Mother's surname, Beatty

K. Mother's age, twenty-one

F. Previous pregnancies, one

K. Father, negro

F. Mother's surname, Mullen

K. Mother's age, fifteen

F. Mother's siblings, none

K. Father, coloured

F. Mother's surname, Rooney

K. Mother's age, forty-two

F. Previous pregnancies, three

K. Father, Nigerian half-caste, raised in institution

Bedsit Land

Children have been able to

>*get their original birth certs*

But sometimes there's very little information on it
And when I talk about child I'm talking about

>*(s)*

>*A woman who's maybe forty*

B ehm
Say Mary Murphy
   Sligo
>*or something*

Or a

   an address in Dublin that's

                  meaning()

Mary Murphy flat 55 B Rathmine

                 Rathmines Road

And this is in 1970

We only had kind of

         temporary addresses

                  in Dublin

You know eh

   bedsit land

Y y you can't (it's)

           just impossible

Bewley's (Twenty Seventeen)

E. Sorry I'm late

J. You're not

E. But were you waiting?

J. I always, I prefer to be a bit early and get a table

E. Looks like they're leaving if the window is better, if you'd prefer to be further from the loo

J. This is better for me, actually

E. Okay, of course

J. Not to, I've some health problems

E. Okay

J. Sorry if that's embarrassing

ACT ONE   147

E. No!

J. I speak my mind

E. I'm jealous

J. Gets me in trouble, my ma used to despair

E. Yeah?

J. Puts everyone on edge she'd say

E. I'd rather you said

J. Yeah?

E. That you were comfortable while we talk, it's a big conversation this

J. And here we are straight into it

E. Are we?

J. This whole, all this goes back to me staying there while I had you

E. Oh

J. Do you want to order something?

E. I'm alright

J. Because I have a pot of tea coming

E. I'll just get a glass of water when it comes

J. We could share I mean, they're big

E. Oh! You enjoy your tea

J. I think it's lovely here but the stairs are murder

E. The windows are gorgeous

J. I saw The Corrs once, sitting over there

E. No way!

J. They're even better looking in the flesh and he's worse

E. I believe it

J. And I saw herself, the young one

E. Who?

J. The, she's Black

E. A famous person?

J. The singer, she did that song that was in the ad for car crashes and she was in the panto there

E. Oh

J. With her brother

E. Samantha Mumba?

J. That's her

E. And Omero

J. She always made me think of you

E. Yeah?

J. Might be why I suggested here

E. Might be

J. That's probably wrong

E. Which?

J. Saying she reminded me, I'm sorry

E. It's, I'm sorry you're not well

J. Ah you manage

E. Still

J. But what I've alway said is, I heard him say I needed stitches and I never got them

E. Oh my god

J. I'm sorry if that's hard to hear

E. I'm, I don't want you to worry about upsetting me

J. Well, it's upsetting and it's your life as well

E. But I don't remember and you do

J. No

Litany Four

C. Mother's surname, Gosson

F. Mother's age, ROTUNDA

C. Previous pregnancies, one

F. Father, Spanish-looking

C. Mother's surname, SISTERS OF CHARITY

F. Mother's age, SISTERS OF CHARITY

C. Mother's siblings, six

F. Father, unknown

C. Mother's surname, TUSLA

F. Mother's age, TUSLA

C. Previous pregnancies, TUSLA

F. Father, TUSLA

Colonies (Oh Three)

K. And there's all this history we're never taught, it's not all Trócaire ads, skinny kids with flies on their eyes, which is way to the east anyway, West Africa had all these huge kingdoms for hundreds and hundreds of years, the Ashanti, the Gonja, Dahomey, and even before them the Mali empire, the Ghana empire, which lasted nearly as long as Rome and you just never hear about it

A. Mad!

K. Except the country's named after it, actually

A. Okay

K. But people don't know, did you know that?

A. No

K. I went myself

A. Oh yeah?

K. Saved up but flights were mad, ended up going as a lay missionary

A. You've faith?

K. Do you?

A. I won't mind if you don't if that's why you're asking

K. I just wanted to see it, but it's gone downhill

A. Since no more kings you mean?

K. Since the Brits, more like, but you can't blame it all on them

A. No?

K. It's gone mad commercial, like what I'd say America is like, money money money, street stalls everywhere, people shouting at you all the time, just go go go non-stop, everyone cramming into these dinky minivans like an under-eighteens hurling team, but they're all strangers, trotros the vans are called and they fucking peg around, sorry

A. I'm shocked

K. Sorry

A. Never heard language like that before

K. No?

A. I'm only messing, they fucking peg around?

K. Yeah, million miles an hour, do your nut trying to drive, and there's beaches but at night people just squat and shit right there in front of you on the ones that aren't private

A. Private beaches?

K. For white people and American Blacks, yeah, and that's the worst thing is everyone thinks you're American

A. Your accent was it?

K. Cos I was working with white people, more, getting paid white money, which to the locals is, what

A. Loads

K. Shitloads, and I'm lighter than them, there's this Twi word obruni yeah?

A. Yeah?

K. Means white person, person who comes in and wrecks everything, like we'd talk about Brits, but I'd hear calling lads me obruni right to my face and they didn't fucking care if I knew

A. Was there anything good?

K. About the place?

A. Or that you came away thinking about, I'm glad I came because that happened

K. I stopped biting my nails?

A. Oh yeah?

K. Cos they kept serving us this pepper soup, and when you dipped fufu in it it stung like, you know

A. Fucking bejaysus

K. Yeah

–

Down the pub the other week, some prick starts in about how the rich Ghanaians, the kings and them, they were the ones capturing poor Africans to sell to the Europeans, turns to me looks me straight in the eye and goes What do you think of that my Nubian friend

A. That's cruel

K. It's fucking bollocks is what it is, it's not true, that's him wanting to get the Brits off the hook so he doesn't have to feel bad about himself

A. He's English?

K. Or he's Church of Ireland, basically the same

A. Right

K. Because when you look at history, when you study like I've studied, you see the way it always goes, Bosnia, Rwanda, the Jews, it's wherever there's a big majority and a small minority, but all the African kingdoms were multicultural all the way back, all the different groups mixing, the Akan the Hausa the Fon the Mandinka, there was never a majority that way, everyone was different but everyone was related

A. Right

K. So I said to him, people turn on their neighbours maybe but not their families

A. –

   You went to college?

K. No?

A. Just you said you'd studied

K. I can read and there's libraries, is what I meant

A. Ah

   –

   When I, when the time came to make the choice I hoped that it meant you'd end up with people who could send you to a good school, that you'd have a degree

K. –

   My brothers are white, are they?

A. Your half-brothers are, yeah

K. Aren't they all?

A. Which?

K. Aren't they all my half-brothers?

A. Joseph isn't

K. So, sorry, you and my dad had another baby?

A. We were married by then

Twenty Eighteen

E. I just wish you'd spoken to us, Nancy

NANCY. Well it's done now

E. Did you fill out a form?

NANCY. I called them and they said to make a written request, yeah

E. Under Freedom of Information?

NANCY. I asked them about GDPR upfront

E. But if it's GDPR you shouldn't have to, did they send you forms to fill out?

NANCY. Yeah

E. And did those forms mention Freedom of Information?

NANCY. Yeah, I think so

E. Okay, fuck, because adoption records are explicitly exempted from Freedom of Information

NANCY. What?

E. GDPR they'll try to invoke privacy in relation to your daughter, they can't tell you anything pertaining to her Just In Case it Somehow causes her harm, but they have to acknowledge your right to make a subject access request, whereas Freedom of Information doesn't apply to adoption information

NANCY. Really?

E. Exception built in for the adoption board and it carried over to TUSLA when they took custodianship of the records, they don't have to tell you anything

NANCY. But I'm not just looking for adoption records, I'm looking for everything they might have on me

E. Like?

NANCY. If you remember, I said before, about – [my situation? my time in the home? the photos]

E. Sorry, yes, the photos, which, I think I said you'll have a hard time getting them to admit that that ever happened, let alone that they still have them

NANCY. Doesn't mean they're not there

E. No, but it does mean that this might not be the route

NANCY. Well, that's what they said back when I tried to go the redress route, so if that's not the route and this isn't the route what is the route?

E. I don't know Nancy, but I hope you find out, I really do

NANCY. Thank you

E. If it's any comfort, I'd imagine they were destroyed

NANCY. Yeah?

E. The liability, that or they're sitting in a box and anyone who knew they were there is dead

NANCY. Can you tell me for sure they were destroyed?

E. No

NANCY. That everyone who saw them is dead?

E. No, Nancy, I can't

NANCY. Then it's not a comfort

Contact Preference (Oh Six)

A. Excuse me eating

F. Not at all

A. On the go since, I don't know

F. First thing?

A. No let-up, yeah, would you like the door closed?

F. I'm alright

ACT ONE   155

A. I might anyway, it's quieter

—

So thank you for coming in

F. Glad to if there's news

A. Well, there is news, but I'm very sorry to say it might not be what you're hoping to hear

F. Okay

A. Which is we made enquiries, and it seems that your mother does not desire contact

F. Okay

A. And in this situation, typically, we say that there is no constructive, no respectful way forward

F. And sorry, was this you?

A. Was which?

F. Did you speak to her?

A. I handled the approach, yes

F. To her?

A. —

What you have to understand is that the contact information I have, you're in your thirties?

F. Thirty-three, yeah

A. Well then, the address the phone number I have is more than thirty years old, so I couldn't get in direct contact even if I wanted to, and I can't go turning up on people's doorsteps

F. But did you speak to my mother?

A. I, it was a discreet approach to family members

F. So you're, or you were able to find, you know who the family is

A. Yes

F. Are, who the family are

A. But it has been made very clear that any further approaches on your behalf are not welcome

F. But would it be different if it was coming from me?

A. How do you mean?

F. If I asked

A. Again, without someone's consent to contact, / the opposite in fact

F. No I know, but do you think the response might be different if it were me myself?

A. It's possible, and what I'd suggest is that you add your name to the contact preference register, / because then if she adds hers

F. I have, I have added my name

A. Well then, you'll know she wants to talk to you the second she adds her name as well

F. But the register is new isn't it? So she might not know, or have had time to, if it's complicated or looked, what, intimidating? We don't know she knows about it for sure, do we? Do we?

A. She would have gotten a leaflet through the door about it, everyone in the country did

F. I didn't

A. –

There have been some problems with the rollout by An Post, / it's true –

F. And what if she moved? If she's in England? America?

A. The government has pledged to do overseas ads every two years

F. An Post are running that too, are they?

A. No

F. Is it actually going to happen?

A. Why wouldn't it?

F. So okay I can't contact her, but can you tell her I'm happy to be contacted?

A. It's, these things are tricky because it'd be a violation of her privacy

F. So you're not allowed ask her if she wants privacy because of her right to privacy?

A. I'm not allowed jump into people's lives with both feet, no, if you imagine for a second, some stranger turning up knowing all about a difficult time in your life, that's a big, it's very scary to have a stranger have that over you, knowing that about you

F. But you do know, whether you tell her or not

A. All the same

Mr X

I mean this is the danger with

    it's like

        it's not natural mothers can register a No Contact preference

    it's natural parents

But fathers weren't named on the birth certs

    so

        how are you going to prove

            that Mr X

                is

s(omeone's) is is is this person's father

    em

> *and what's to stop anybody rocking*
> *up and*

> *registering a no contact preference*

> (*Breath and laugh.*)

> > *you know*

> *How are you gonna h(ow)*

> > *how are you going to r(eally) verify it*

> > > *you know*

Glasgow (Twenty Fifteen)

J. But after Glasgow it was down to London and there's Black people just everywhere and I'm a bit of a hit with men, Black men, and I've never, growing up I didn't have much to do with boys, didn't like me and I knew or, I'd learned not to trust them, but now all of a sudden because I'm light and still had a bit of my accent so men, Caribbean men, always thought I was Bajan or Belizean or Jamaican, three four years there I don't think I paid into a club once cos all the lads on the doors fancied me, which looking back is wild because do you know what I don't think I ever got my hair done before that? Never learned growing up cos the only time they even combed our hair as kids was with paraffin for nits, big steel comb and going at it so hard so hard and dry your hair's coming out in clumps, blood on your scalp half the time and you're not sure if you're bleeding or if it's the things, mad looking back, but pushing thirty and there I was washing my hair with shampoo from the corner shop, REEFING it back in two big bunches soaking wet, like Mickey Mouse with an even fuckeder hairline, might be why I still didn't have many friends, always a bit of a loner me, until Es arrived, which was eighty-eight? But then it's easy, you just go to the raves and have a nice time and if someone kisses you you let them, sublet my room to a truck driver cos half the week I wasn't there I was coming down in some manky bedroom belonging to a white boy with a Bob poster, and then Lee was born and it was that made me want to know, I think, so I could tell him and it'd be different for him, so I wrote the nuns a letter asking about my parents and they said *We're sorry we've nothing, no information,* so I said okay, and I didn't think about it again until Lee died, killed himself I should say, which was, beg your pardon, fucksake, you must be mortified

T. No!

J. I didn't want to cry

T. Take your time

J. –

But that's what got me interested in trying to find you again, why I did the DNA thing, all that and that film *Philomena*, did you see it?

T. No! Good?

J. Beautiful, I cried my eyes out, my friend didn't know what to do

T. Wow

J. And I thought, if it could happen for her, if there are ways to do it without having to ask the nuns

T. Right

J. Or the social workers, now, I think it is, TUSLA and them, which is, sorry that's half my life, but is why it took so long, years, to find you all

T. She really wanted to meet you

J. Yeah?

T. Not just at the end but, if she didn't for those years it was because she was shy, she would have been scared you didn't want to

J. Meet?

T. Yeah

J. But I did

T. And we know now that it wasn't, I'm so sorry you were looking so long, but from where we were we'd never heard from you

J. I know

T. And when she asked, because she did ask, but when she asked they told her you had been adopted

J. –

   So I'm your aunt am I?

T. Yeah, weird

J. Is it?

T. Or just new, she only had brothers

J. Okay

T. Or that's what we thought

J. So I'm special

T. Yeah

J. –

   You know, my dad was Yoruba

T. Yeah?

J. So in his culture, you should do a little bow thing to me

T. Now?

J. When we meet, because I'm your elder

T. –

   Are you asking me to?

Mormons Redux (Twenty Thirteen)

K. Have you tried the Mormons?

E. Why?

K. In Glasnevin, they have really good records

E. Of people who were Mormons?

K. No everyone

E. Why?

K. Wherever they go they do big family trees so they can baptise their ancestors and be together in heaven

E. What?

K. Their ancestors who died before there were Mormons, because it's so new

E. Right

K. Mormonism, they baptised Anne Frank a while back there

E. Fuck off

K. And four hundred thousand other Jews who died in the Holocaust

E. Fucksake

K. So they might have you original birth cert

E. Is that allowed?

K. I don't know but it's true

Brunches (Twenty Twenty-One)

T. But okay, it's going well so I'm invited back

K. Okay

T. So we go back

K. Okay

T. And not to be all *I'm a fucking sexbomb*

K. No

T. But everyone involved is having a really good time

K. Okay

T. Like, in the taxi but sneakily because that's not fair

K. No

T. Right, he didn't ask for that, nice guy, Black guy, but that and in the stairs bit on the way up, the, what's it called

K. Stairwell

T. The stairwell, and while the keys are coming out, the whole time

K. Okay

T. But then I get in

K. Oh?

T. The door

K. Yeah

T. But we get in the door and it's shoes off

K. Okay

T. Which fair enough

K. Yeah

T. Normal enough, yeah?

K. Yeah

ACT ONE   163

T. Especially Nigerians is what I hear, and Asians, from friends who are, so no shocks there, actually more normal if you think about it, you know, globally

K. I wouldn't know

T. Oh yeah?

K. Because, my dad was Nigerian yeah but I was fostered

T. Right, okay, but the point is it's also socks off

K. At the door?

T. At the door

K. The fuck?

T. Right?

K. Where do they go?

T. The socks?

K. Is there a rack, or – ?

T. There's a line of shoes, and they all have socks in them

K. Jaysus

T. But that's weird, right?

K. Fucking weird

T. And they're all Adidas

K. Like, fun exaggeration all or – ?

T. No like all all, there's like eight pairs of shoes and they're all, stripes stripes stripes

K. Fuck

T. Twenty-four stripes

K. Yeah

T. Maths

K. Fair play

T. Which I'm, I'm on my best behaviour

K. Of course

T. So no comment, whatever gets the boat floating you know

K. Yeah

T. But then the floor is fucking manky

K. No way

T. Crumbs and mad shit

K. Sake

T. Like, we get to the bed and my feet are like, covered

K. Jesus

T. Filthy

K. Yeah

T. And I'm trying to behave like, okay, you do bare fucking feet but don't fucking sweep, that's fine, but then you know that move where she runs her foot up your leg?

K. Like, when – ?

T. You're on top yeah

K. Yeah

T. But I'm down to my jocks so it's on my bare skin and it feels, it's cold as well so it's like someone is running two Brunches up and down my leg

K. Jesus

T. The ice creams

K. No I know

T. So not sexy

K. No

T. Like what's that about?

K. I mean

T. Yeah?

ACT ONE   165

K. It's fucking something

—

So you're single?

T. No?

K. Oh

T. Married a year and a half

K. Right

T. No kids yet but we're trying

K. Haven't missed any nieces or nephews being born!

T. Oh yeah

K. Or have I?

T. My sister has one

K. Okay

T. Iris

K. Beautiful name

T. —

The ma just needs time

K. Yeah?

T. I think that's what's hard for her is, she feels like, she doesn't want it to look like she's more interested in one of us, because what are you?

K. What am I?

T. Seventy-eight? Seventy-nine?

K. Like what year was I born?

T. Cos we could be twins

K. Yeah!

T. If I was Black

K. Yeah

T. And I'm eighty

K. Seventy-seven here

T. So three years older

K. Yeah

T. Gone forty

K. Yeah

T. You don't look it, Black don't crack and all that

K. Cos forty's fucking ancient is it?

T. You tell me, but us meeting as well is, this today, might not help

K. –

T. No?

K. I don't mean THAT we met, just now I've met you, it might be weird for her that we're so alike

T. Physically?

K. And personality, everything

T. Yeah?

Mormons Reredux (Twenty Twenty-One)

J. Have you tried the Mormons?

K. Fuck that, I need or the COUNTRY needs another bunch of religious weirdos taking control of vital state infrastructure with no oversight, hey Ireland should you be keeping track of all these vulnerable children and their paperworks, I don't know probably hahaha, looks like the God people have it covered hahaha, we need that like we need a fucking hole in the fucking head

J. But if that's the only place

K. That has it?

J. Or where you'll be able to access it, yeah

K. I don't need to know that much

J. Yeah?

K. And I shouldn't have to ask this much

J. I know

Litany Five

E. 1960

C. Dublin

E. Christ the King

C. Mary Jane Fagan May 14th

E. Dublin

C. The Most Precious Blood

E. Elizabeth Gillick July 16th

C. Ferns

E. Horeswood

C. Thomas Pender July 23rd

E. Kildare and Leighlin

C. Two Mile House

E. Ellen Hanaphy August 13th

C. Armagh

E. Holy Family

C. Denis Earley August 13th

E. Ferns

C. Our Lady's Island

E. Margaret Tatterson August 13th

C. Great name

E. Tatterson?

C. Also what are the chances?

E. Of what?

C. Three in a row, August 13th

E. This is baptisms not birthdays though

C. Oh yeah

E. They did them, do them, in batches like

C. Oh yeah

Litany Six

J. Mother's surname, TUSLA

C. Date of birth, TUSLA

J. Name of child, TUSLA

C. Place of birth, TUSLA

J. Your name, TUSLA

C. My name, TUSLA

J. My age, TUSLA

C. My star sign, TUSLA

J. TUSLA's phone number, TUSLA

C. Favourite colour, TUSLA

J. Favourite film, TUSLA

C. TUSLA, TUSLA

J. TUSLA, TUSLA

C. TUSLA

J. TUSLA

C. TUSLA

J. TUSLA

Twenty Sixteen

NANCY. I saw you in the local paper, / and then your number was on your website

ALICE. / They're very good, they cover everything /

NANCY. And I really like the sound of this piece you're doing with the actors, where you fill in the blank spaces in redacted documents with the names of the organisations who redacted them

ALICE. Thanks, I was worried it was a bit On The Nose, but you know, if Jenny Holzer can get away with it because she's white and straight

NANCY. And when it said you were adopted I thought, maybe you've looked into your birth family already, have you?

ALICE. I tried, anyway

NANCY. And got nothing?

ALICE. Yeah

NANCY. Okay, because what I think is, I think I might be your mother

–

ALICE. Oh

NANCY. Birth mother, which is, it sounds wild I know

ALICE. Just a bit

NANCY. And I might be jumping the gun a bit with this, I've been trying to find out officially and it keeps being Wait And See, Wait And See, Fuck Off And Die, and then I open the paper and you're there, and there's your age, and the African name put me off but then when you said you chose it yourself

ALICE. I don't really know what to say to that

NANCY. Because your, if the man I had my second baby with was your father, he was like me

ALICE. Like you how?

NANCY. He, I was never adopted and neither was he

ALICE. Okay

NANCY. Fostered out a bit, here and there, but industrial schools mostly

ALICE. Okay, fuck

NANCY. Which was, it wasn't the only reason but it was sort of why we couldn't keep you

ALICE. If it was me

NANCY. If it was you, why we couldn't keep the baby is all I meant, because neither of us had anyone

ALICE. Okay

NANCY. And that was why he didn't have an African name, he didn't know his parents, so I wondered about you until the interview said you'd chosen – [Olanrewaju]

ALICE. Olanrewaju

NANCY. What does it mean?

ALICE. My wealth is the future

NANCY. Planning on hitting it big?

ALICE. More like, there's nothing in the past for me, in my family or – [any of that? Any of this?]

NANCY. Fair enough

ALICE. Feels a bit silly now if you're right and my dad wasn't Nigerian like they told me

NANCY. It's beautiful

ACT ONE   171

ALICE. And sorry, you called him, you said your second baby?

NANCY. Yes

ALICE. So if we're, if you're my mother I have a brother or a sister?

NANCY. I should have, they died

ALICE. I'm sorry

NANCY. Funny how everyone's driven demented with that now, isn't it?

ALICE. Which?

NANCY. They, gender-neutral language, people not identifying as one or the other, like that's new

ALICE. Yeah, hilarious

NANCY. I struggle with it sometimes, it's classic, you're so conscious of not being the Grumpy Old Lesbian Who Doesn't Get The Kids that you fuck up and make yourself look like – [you know]

ALICE. The Grumpy Old Lesbian

NANCY. Yeah

ALICE. You're gay?

NANCY. Is that – [okay? a problem?]

ALICE. Yes! I'm gay

NANCY. No way!

ALICE. Card-carrying

NANCY. You wouldn't think that'd be genetic, would you, or we'd die out

ALICE. Assuming we're related

NANCY. Assuming, yes

–

But I did it no problem there

ALICE. Which?

NANCY. They died, I said, but then it's easy I suppose because I don't actually know if my baby was, I never got to see them

–

ALICE. I'm sorry, I don't want to be rude, but I'm finding this really hard and weird

NANCY. It is really hard and weird

ALICE. And I don't want to sound, but do you have any way of us finding out for sure, of us confirming?

NANCY. Do you have a birthmark on your left leg?

–

ALICE. Nancy, wasn't it?

NANCY. That's me, yeah

ALICE. Yeah, Nancy, I do

NANCY. Okay

–

Okay then

As the act ends, we're suddenly in a gallery space in 2021. If there was a curtain, this is accomplished by a curtain drop. The voices are in a recognisable world for a loaded moment before blackout.

ACT TWO

A gallery space in Dublin's north inner city. Not particularly fancy. ALICE's *art pieces are up around the walls and throughout the space – crucial to the execution of this act is that the piece entitled* Pende *is a sealed-off space within the space.* NANCY *is trying not to be conspicuous watching the face-off between* ALICE *and* ANNA. THOMAS *is genuinely oblivious as he physically warms up: maybe he's in downward dog position.*

ALICE. I just think that if YOU ask ME, hey, would you like the performance parts to be interpreted, my assumption is that you're offering to get us an ISL interpreter, / not saying YOU should get one

ANNA. I did offer to, I did offer that

ALICE. Right, but we're supposed to pay her, even though we didn't budget for it, and you saw the budget and / didn't say anything at that point, so it's a little –

ANNA. You didn't mention live performance, live performance under COVID safety conditions by the way, until like two weeks ago, Alice

ALICE. –

But if you invited me to dinner and then I turned up at your house and you were expecting me to go through your fridge and do the actual, you know, cooking of the dinner, that'd be weird right?

ANNA. –

I really fought for you to be able to have performers in here

ALICE. I know

ANNA. Because when I first said it to Marion, I know you're grateful that she okayed the show / in the first place –

ALICE. / Not THAT grateful, not that big a deal for me /

ANNA. but she was just pull the plug, absolutely not, / more hassle than it's worth

ALICE. I know, I know she was

ANNA. And it's me did all the COVID compliance, policy, tests, I mean it was me got down and taped the floor, I was sweeping up after you when the cleaner couldn't come in

ALICE. Another thing I have heard you say

ANNA. So tell you what, she's on her way, you talk to her

ALICE. Marion?

ANNA. The interpreter, I got her here to talk to you, if you think you shouldn't be the one to pay her why don't you say it to her face?

ANNA *exits*.

ALICE (*after her*). Thanks Anna

NANCY. You hate her

ALICE. I don't hate them

–

Is it that obvious?

NANCY (*quoting*). Them?

ALICE (*clarifying*). Or she, because Of Course – [they use both They/She]

NANCY. What, does she sell drugs to children?

ALICE. If only, they're just –

NANCY. Yeah?

ALICE. I'm not being fair

NANCY. So?

ALICE. –

But they're a human bottle of vodka with a rainbow flag on it

NANCY. Which is bad?

ALICE. Like the nails, always has their nails done in pink and purple and blue but one hundred per cent has a secret white finance boyfriend and would shit their pants if you actually tried to touch their fanny, just a total sexless commodifier who thinks queerness is an aesthetic not a struggle, is that mean?

THOMAS/NANCY. Yeah

ALICE (*remembering him*). Tom, how you doing over there?

THOMAS. Fine, but I can leave if yous want

NANCY. Not me

ALICE. Tom, can we chat about the singing for a sec?

THOMAS *wraps up his warm-up.*

THOMAS. Hit me

ALICE. I want to!

THOMAS. You didn't like the singing

ALICE. Because I know it's improv, but it's structured improv

THOMAS. It was, I was going with it

ALICE. What were you going with?

THOMAS. There was an energy

ALICE. From who?

THOMAS. From, you know, the exchange, me and her, and sorry, we – (*Meaning* NANCY.) haven't properly had a, are you working on this as well?

ALICE. No

NANCY. I don't need to be here, if you'd rather –

THOMAS. Just I didn't know we'd be doing notes before tonight, and in front of everyone

ALICE. One person, in front of one person, and since you'd to run / straight after the playtest yesterday

THOMAS. Childminder, I was on pick-up

ALICE. I know, Tom, but if the night before we open you're still, can we go through it?

THOMAS. Now?

ALICE. The scripted bits, even, please

THOMAS (*scripted*). This piece is called *Pende*, the name of both a people and its language.

(*Breaking off.*) I'm feeling quite exposed here

NANCY. I'll go

THOMAS. I don't mind you being here

ALICE (*to* NANCY). Two minutes

THOMAS. It's being watched is all

ALICE (*to* THOMAS). You're an actor

THOMAS. Watching notes though, it's like showering with someone

ALICE. –

How?

THOMAS. Makes you self-conscious, am I going too fast, taking too long, shampoo first or soap, is it weird to go for your asscrack, or if you DON'T – (*To* NANCY.) do you want to step in even?

NANCY. To the – [performance? thing?]

THOMAS. Run it with me, yeah – (*To* ALICE.) cos if it's the improv is the problem –

ALICE (*to* NANCY). You really don't have to

NANCY. I'd like to

ALICE. –

Okay then

THOMAS *stands by the closed* Pende *chamber. Solemn. Performance energy.* NANCY *faces him.*

THOMAS. This piece is called *Pende*, the name of both a people and its language.

It imagines a world where art is community and community is art and neither is a product.

The Pende people make beautiful art, then hide it for years.

You can ask me about this piece, but I don't have to tell you.

NANCY. Okay

THOMAS. And you can ask to see this piece, but I don't have to show you.

Which is one meaning of community.

NANCY. Okay

–

Hi

THOMAS. Hi

NANCY. Thomas?

THOMAS. Tom

NANCY. Tom what?

THOMAS. Alkhatib

NANCY. And what's that?

ALICE. Jesus

NANCY (*to* ALICE). What?

ALICE. Nothing, it's probably good practice / for – [you? (THOMAS) later? white ladies?]

THOMAS. It's Palestinian

NANCY. Can I see the piece?

THOMAS. –

No

NANCY. Okay

THOMAS. –

You're Nancy yeah?

NANCY. Nancy Earley

THOMAS. And what has you here?

ALICE. Is this the piece?

NANCY. Need a chat with herself

THOMAS. What about?

NANCY. Think I'd get in trouble

ALICE. Don't act like, I never asked you not to say

THOMAS. Do you want to say?

NANCY. Yes

THOMAS. So say

NANCY. I'm her mother

THOMAS. Fuck off

ALICE. Birth mother

NANCY. Birth mother

THOMAS. Since when?

NANCY. –

   Since she was born?

THOMAS. But have you known, though

ALICE. Few years, can we not – [stop? continue? do anything else?]

NANCY (*conciliatory*). Tell me about the piece

THOMAS (*making a point for* ALICE *of his segue*). Well, first maybe you should tell me what you already know about the Pende people

NANCY. Fuck-all

THOMAS. So why do you want to see it then?

NANCY. Because she made it

THOMAS. Fair enough, but does that give you the right?

ACT TWO 179

NANCY. So I've to pay?

THOMAS. No

NANCY. Is the joke that there's nothing in there?

ALICE. It's not a joke

THOMAS (*working very hard to make it not sound hard*). This is community, this is two people in an exchange that can't be short-cutted by power, money, / orders, police

ALICE. Short-circuited

THOMAS. Fuck, short-circuited

NANCY. So I've to convince you

THOMAS. Yeah

NANCY. Can I see the piece if I let you sing for me?

ALICE (*to* NANCY). Come on

THOMAS. That's pretty much what happened yesterday

ALICE. She asked you did you want to sing for her

THOMAS. Yeah

ALICE. Out of nowhere

THOMAS. I might have mentioned

ALICE. That you wanted to sing?

THOMAS. That I'm a person who sings

NANCY. What song?

THOMAS *should sing something brief but musical theatre-y and ostentatious at this point; it doesn't have to be the 'I'M READY NOW' from 'Marry Me A Little', but that would be perfect.*

ALICE. And is that what we're doing here?

THOMAS. –

Yeah? Like you keep saying, people not things, relationships not transactions, remind them I'm a person

ALICE. But in your words, if a journalist asks, what is this

THOMAS. That we're doing?

ALICE. Do YOU think, yeah

THOMAS. Well it's Malorie Blackman, the, *Noughts and Crosses* and them, we always have to wait to be invited everywhere, how would they like it if it was the other way around

ALICE. White people

THOMAS. Yeah

ALICE. And you not privately inviting someone to view a private artwork unless they let you sing a song, that's qualitatively comparable to apartheid is it?

THOMAS. Yeah? Gets you thinking like

THOMAS*'s phone goes.*

ALICE. Yeah Tom, but we want them thinking about imperialism, not about how great you'd be as the first Palestinian Bobby in *Company*

–

Yeah Tom?

THOMAS. Sorry, this is the minder

THOMAS *takes a call as he leaves the room.* ALICE *and* NANCY *are alone.*

ALICE. Fucking actors

NANCY. I like him

ALICE. I'm going to say something

NANCY. Go on then

ALICE. If I could do it with middle-class drama-school white people I would

NANCY. Yeah?

ALICE. Because they're so guilty so, pat me on the head and tell me I'm One Of The Good Ones, you send them a PDF they actually fucking read it

NANCY. You're nervous

ALICE. A short PDF, six pages, for tonight you mean?

NANCY. First time with an actual audience, no?

ALICE. A whole five people at a time wearing masks, but yeah

NANCY. So it's natural

ALICE. I'm not nervous I'm, I meant it when I said I was busy

NANCY. I can see that

ALICE. So if you could, / you said you had something to say

NANCY. What's the story with this one [these]?

A graphic piece (or pieces) which is a subversion of the UDHR (Universal Declaration of Human Rights). It might say, for example: 13. YOU HAVE THE RIGHT TO DROWN IN THE MEDITERRANEAN, or 13. YOU HAVE THE RIGHT TO BE MURDERED IN YOUR HOME, or 14. YOU HAVE THE RIGHT TO HANG YOURSELF IN MOSNEY, or 8. YOU HAVE THE RIGHT TO BE SUED BANKRUPT

ALICE. –

Universal human rights require a universal power to enforce them, it's empire with a halo painted on it

NANCY. You like that phrase

ALICE. Which?

NANCY. Bad Things with Good Things painted on them

ALICE. That's lots of Things

NANCY. And you're, you think human rights are A Bad Thing

ALICE. I haven't done the reading but I like all the anarchists I know, so – [it follows? You know?]

NANCY. Skips or Bookchin?

ALICE. Sorry?

NANCY. I was in squats a lot in London when I went over first, and with the anarchists it was always either one woman skip-diving and doing the 'mutual'-aid meal-runs on her own and helping in eight soup kitchens until she got scurvy, or three lads who never shut up about Murray Bookchin and stole your beer

ALICE. There are Black anarchist thinkers, / you know,

NANCY. / I'm sure, but never my bag /

ALICE. And I didn't think you'd think hierarchy was A Good Thing

NANCY. Hierarchy no, rules yes – I think I said to you before, growing up, the nun we hated the most was the one who made it up as she went along

ALICE. You did

NANCY. It was her knocked out these two [teeth] on this side

ALICE. Fuck

NANCY. She'd strip you for doing something she'd told you to do the day before, whereas the ones who tried to follow the rules –

ALICE. Yeah?

NANCY. Well, they were awful too but sometimes they'd get embarrassed

ALICE. –

Is it insensitive – [to ask?]

NANCY. Yeah?

ALICE (*quoting*). She'd strip you?

NANCY. The hide off you, I meant

ALICE. Okay

NANCY. But that too

ALICE. –

Okay

CIARA *enters with a tote with two lunchboxes in it.*

Hi?

CIARA. Are you the artist?

ALICE. You're the interpreter

CIARA. Yeah

ALICE. Ciara

CIARA. That's me!

ALICE. Brilliant, upfront, did Anna talk to you about payment?

CIARA. We, I work through an agency so the rates are standard

ALICE. But our problem, I meant

CIARA. No?

ALICE. That she's trying to offload your fee to us at the last minute, which, you know, I'm not loving Tee Bee Haitch

CIARA. –

Right

ALICE. Very Waged behaviour, you definitely know the way

CIARA. Is she waged?

ALICE. Or, she's not freelance / is all I mean

CIARA. But it's your show isn't it?

ALICE. Yes, I'm Alice, did I not say?

CIARA. No

ALICE. Sorry

CIARA. But what I meant was, the gallery didn't commission the show

ALICE. No

CIARA. They're just hosting it

ALICE. Yeah

CIARA. So why would they pay me? That's like, you invite me out for drinks and the bar is supposed to give us our drinks for free just because you booked a table?

KING and EDWARD enter with ANNA close behind. Moment of recognition between ANNA and CIARA.

ALICE. –

One second?

CIARA. Sure

ALICE (*to* EDWARD). Have you heard from Funmi?

EDWARD. She says she's sorry, here soon

ALICE. For real?

EDWARD. How should I know?

KING. Did you see around the corner?

ALICE. It's half, King

KING. And that's On Me, but did you see?

ALICE. Which?

KING. Around the cottages, big eviction, like fifty sixty people there, neighbours and union heads, private security, four Garda cars

ALICE. Fuck

ANNA. I wanted to ask about that

ALICE. Ask what?

ANNA. Because if it keeps going our audience can't get to us

ALICE. –

Will it?

EDWARD. Unless the tenants reach an agreement with the landlord

ALICE. So we're fucked

EDWARD. Maybe

ANNA. Have a look yourself, your call if we're cancelling

ALICE. One second – (*To* NANCY.) do you want to go get yourself a coffee or – [take a walk? leave and never come back?]

NANCY. I don't mind waiting

ALICE. Okay, but, I can't promise you a minute in the next hour

NANCY. That's fine

ALICE. –

Okay – (*To* CIARA.) and are you – [good to go? set up? ready?]

CIARA. Is there a script I could be looking at?

ALICE. Script, right

CIARA. It's easiest, I can see spellings

ALICE. Hard copy?

CIARA. Ideally!

ANNA. You don't have the script?

KING. I've the link to the version on the drive here? (*Phone*.)

ALICE. Doesn't have the rehearsal edits, / haven't had time

ANNA. Because I did say in an email, / if you need to print I've to go home

ALICE. Yes, you said, you said lots of things – (*To* KING.) King will you get Thomas, and can you go through the scripted parts with –

CIARA/ANNA. Ciara

ALICE. With Ciara, sorry

KING. Where is he?

ALICE. Out the back 'talking to the minder'

KING. OH, then do I've time for a smoke as well?

ALICE. King – [OBVIOUSLY not? come on? you're killing me?]

KING. Teeny tiny quick one – (*To* EDWARD.) will you be gone – [when I come back]?

EDWARD. Yeah

KING. I'll be over soon

He kisses EDWARD *goodbye and exits with* CIARA.

ALICE (*to* EDWARD). Over where soon?

ANNA (*to* ALICE). So do you want hard copies?

ALICE. What?

ANNA. Am I hopping on my bike to go home and print a script Ciara can actually use? / Because I don't think it's fair

ALICE. Great thanks so much for that Anna I'll email it to you in a minute seeya soon bye

ANNA. –

ANNA *exits*.

EDWARD. You HATE her

ALICE (*to* EDWARD). What has you here?

EDWARD. So I know you've said you don't want the comms role any more –

ALICE. Edward, baby, my bestie, my comrade, tell me you're not coming to me with union business right now

EDWARD. But we haven't had the chance to elect your replacement yet, / so for the moment it's still you

ALICE. / Six weeks, Ed, it's been six weeks /

EDWARD. because we can't have meetings, and this eviction, this is BIG

ALICE. I don't live in this postcode any more, / it's why I quit

EDWARD. There's people from all the branches coming, / and we're going to need EVERYBODY

ALICE. / So why do you need me? /

EDWARD. and we're going to need coverage as well, pile on the pressure before people start drifting off, and you have more Twitter followers than any of the union accounts by, like, thousands, on an account that isn't tied to your real name

ALICE. Because we're all going to get arrested?

EDWARD. Have a look babes!

ALICE. I'm going to

EDWARD. Because it's ugly, it's really fucking ugly, seven this morning private security burst in and start smashing things, only way to make them stop is to leave the house

ALICE/NANCY. Fuckers

The unison is unexpected.

EDWARD. –

Is that news to you?

ALICE. They still there?

EDWARD. Security?

ALICE. Yeah

EDWARD. Yeah, in the house, won't leave while we've people outside

ALICE. Good

EDWARD. Only we have the Gardaí trying to move us on because us standing in the street – (*Quoting.*) Isn't COVID Safe

ALICE. Fucksake

EDWARD. So public attention would be a good thing to have, embarrass them out of it

ALICE. Security lads in the house get to stay though?

EDWARD. That's – (*Quoting.*) Between The Landlord And The Tenant

ALICE. Of course, and did they get the locks?

EDWARD. Like did they change them?

ALICE. Yeah

EDWARD. First thing, and you know who it is?

ALICE. Who who is?

EDWARD. The tenants

ALICE. No?

> FUNMI *enters. She goes to kiss* ALICE, *who subtly pulls back.* FUNMI *is taken aback,* ALICE *is conscious of* NANCY *and* EDWARD *being there.*

FUNMI. I'm sorry I'm late?

NANCY. This is your girlfriend?

ALICE. My partner, yeah

NANCY. Sorry

FUNMI. I prefer girlfriend

ALICE. Girlfriend then

FUNMI. I'm not a cowboy

ALICE. And this, this is Nancy

FUNMI. Oh

NANCY. Yeah

FUNMI. That's you!

NANCY. That's me

ALICE. I've to – [step out? go?]

EDWARD. You go look

ALICE. You coming?

EDWARD. I can wait till you've made up your mind

ALICE. –

Everyone's so patient today, I'm so lucky

> ALICE *leaves* NANCY *alone with* FUNMI *and* EDWARD.

NANCY (*to* FUNMI). You're a poet!

FUNMI. She told you!

NANCY. I can't wait to hear something

EDWARD. No pressure

NANCY. I love Audre Lorde!

ACT TWO   189

EDWARD. What?

FUNMI. Me too!

NANCY. And ye are brother and sister?

FUNMI. Sadly

EDWARD. Bitch

NANCY. –

  So many gays!

FUNMI. –

  Apologies?

NANCY. No it's great, I mean

EDWARD. Good

NANCY. Makes me really happy

FUNMI. Amen

NANCY. I mean I'm A Gay myself, so – [thumbs-up? no big deal?]

FUNMI. Okay!

NANCY. From way back, she never said?

FUNMI. No

NANCY. Militant, not Political

EDWARD. Yay?

NANCY. I mean not A Political Lesbian but very political political, I'm bringing this up loads today but when I was in London first I shaved my head and had everyone calling me Angel for three years

FUNMI. I love it

EDWARD. Why Angel?

NANCY. Beloved of God, both male and female, I was twenty and light-headed from all the patchouli?

FUNMI. I LOVE IT

NANCY. Lots of that on the go

FUNMI. Yeah?

NANCY. Still illegal to be gay over here, remember, so loads of queers on that scene over there, plus hot water, running water even, was a bit of a coin toss, everyone was a bit hairy and Perfumed and ambiguous

FUNMI. How long was that for?

NANCY. The squatting?

FUNMI. Oh you were squatting?

NANCY. Because, that first place only six months but overall five or six years

FUNMI. I just thought cheap shithole, and I mean this in a nice way okay?

NANCY. I'm scared!

FUNMI. But you don't look like you lived in squats for years

NANCY. Thanks?

FUNMI. Or even like you could be Alice's mum

EDWARD. How's that work?

FUNMI. Ed

NANCY. Which?

EDWARD. You know, you're a gay Angel but you're Alice's – [mother]

FUNMI. ED

EDWARD. And I know it's not only married mammies and daddies have babies, / but you said it was the eighties, so – [gay with kids?]

FUNMI. Ed oh my god be silent

EDWARD. Sorry

NANCY. It's fine! All I can say is, life is long

EDWARD. Fingers crossed

ACT TWO   191

NANCY. –

(*To* FUNMI.) Do you love her?

FUNMI. –

Alice?

NANCY. Cheeky of me

FUNMI. Bit cheeky

EDWARD. But do you?

FUNMI. Ed – [What the fuck?]

NANCY. I'm sorry, I don't even really mean, you don't have to CONFESS

FUNMI. No?

NANCY. It just makes me happy to think ye're together, solid, that you both have someone to look after you

FUNMI. We're in it

NANCY. Yeah?

FUNMI. All the way!

NANCY. Brill

EDWARD. Is that a yes?

FUNMI. Yes, it's a yes

EDWARD. Because you still haven't said it

FUNMI. I love her

NANCY. I'm happy for her, for ye

EDWARD. Just don't ask if they're getting married

NANCY. Last thing I'd ever do!

EDWARD. So it runs in the family!

NANCY. –

Is there a bathroom?

FUNMI. Through there, the door doesn't lock

NANCY. And I might actually grab a coffee or – [something? leave and never come back?]

But lovely meeting you both

NANCY *exits.* EDWARD *and* FUNMI *are left alone. She stares him out of it.*

–

EDWARD. What?

FUNMI. Edward Isaac

EDWARD. Oluwafunmilayo

FUNMI. What is going on?

EDWARD. Ashawo

FUNMI. Says you

EDWARD. That's her mum

FUNMI. Birth mother

EDWARD. And?

FUNMI. And?

EDWARD. You're FLIRTING

FUNMI. I'm CHARMING

EDWARD. You are FLIRTING

FUNMI. A little

EDWARD. Trying to collect the full set?

FUNMI. I want her to like me

EDWARD. You want her to lick you

FUNMI. You don't flirt with King's mum?

EDWARD. I don't LOOK at King's mum

FUNMI. So let me live my LIFE

EDWARD. Just don't knock either of them up

FUNMI. Stick a needle in my eye

EDWARD. Because I'm too young to be an auntie

FUNMI. Bitch you're twenty-six

EDWARD. Twenty-five and eleven-twelfths, REPENT sinner

FUNMI. Whatever

–

Did you say it to her?

EDWARD. Alice?

FUNMI. About – [you know], yeah

EDWARD. Didn't get a chance

They spot ALICE *re-entering.*

FUNMI. Ed

EDWARD. I said I'd try

(*To* ALICE.) So?

ALICE. Fuckers, it's horrible

EDWARD. Then I'll see you over there? Sooner is better, I know you think your Art is Very Important, but – [this is more important]

EDWARD *exits.*

FUNMI. You okay?

ALICE. You are so late

FUNMI. Goddess

ALICE. What do you want

FUNMI. Sweet goddess I love more than I love life

ALICE. Tell me you're not going to try and flake

–

You're flaking?

FUNMI *is moving toward* ALICE *who is moving back.*

FUNMI. You still feeling shy?

ALICE. Because today has been, I really really / REALLY don't need another thing

FUNMI. Today, you're right, TODAY, UGH, and my question is, what does a woman have to do to get a kiss Today

ALICE *kisses* FUNMI.

I'm sorry you're stressed

ALICE. Are you going to make it worse?

FUNMI. King said he'd say to you

ALICE. Yeah?

FUNMI. And Ed, both of them so you'd know it's important, because it's Richie

ALICE. What is?

FUNMI. Being evicted

ALICE. Poetry Richie?

FUNMI. And what's-her-name, used to be with Tom, turns everything into a question

ALICE. Richie's with JILL?

FUNMI. Nearly two years

ALICE. No way

FUNMI. Since, like, right after Tom

ALICE. This fucking city

FUNMI. And the show, I know it's important to you, important, full stop, but why can't we open tomorrow?

ALICE. Why does it have to be you, or, us? The crowd's already, / there's fucking shitloads of people there

FUNMI. Until people start needing to pee, then it's leave to find a loo or see what happens when you squat behind a Garda car, / they're already looking for excuses, taking names, threatening fines

ALICE. / Yeah, okay, I get it /

FUNMI. We'll still be here tomorrow, all the stuff / will still be here

ALICE (*quoting*). Stuff!

FUNMI. All the ART, everything we need will still be here but Richie might not be

ALICE. –

They talk the talk really well here, and they pretend to have done the reading, even Marion, but they've never programmed an artist like me on their own before

FUNMI. I know

ALICE. I don't want to fuck it up

FUNMI. I know

ALICE. Give them an excuse not to again, Oh We Tried That And It Didn't Work

FUNMI. I know

ALICE. Because the headfuck of, did I do something that pissed them off, did they lose interest when I did new stuff, or was it all bullshit and they were never really interested at all, and you can't Just Ask so you never know for sure

FUNMI. The fucking worst

ALICE. I don't want to be the reason someone else feels that way

FUNMI. Even if that, if they're shit that's not on you

ALICE. And I've got enough things I'll never know, you know?

FUNMI. I do

–

But fuck them get yours, right?

ALICE. Yeah

FUNMI. Plus I'm more of a volunteer than an Employee, / so – [if you think about it, I should be allowed flake, DUH]

ALICE. Are you?

FUNMI. Yeah? I'm doing your show even though that's not my thing, / I'm not paid, I'm volunteering

ALICE. You're a performer

FUNMI. I'm a poet

ALICE. And you perform your poems, so how is this – (*Exaggerated.*) Not Your Thing

FUNMI. One it's dialogue, two I didn't write it, three I'm only doing it because I love you and no one you auditioned for your performance about Africans was actually From Africa

ALICE. That's not the, that's not why I asked you

FUNMI. That isn't what A Balance of Performer Experience Means? Tallaght Ghanaian, Belfast Palestinian, actually lived in Abuja but only until I was eight?

ALICE. No it means A Balance of Performer Experiences

FUNMI. Plus the big one, you're not paying me

ALICE. Oh don't do that, like it's – [unfair? unethical? a gender thing? sexist?]

FUNMI. I'm not Doing That, it IS That, you're not paying me and you're paying King and Tom, so either I'm a volunteer and I can leave when I want or you're an evil boss, which is it? What's the story?

ALICE. The story is, I saw this coming

FUNMI. –

Excuse me?

ALICE. It's, I'm paying them because I can count on them, I knew you'd do something like this

FUNMI. Something like what?

ALICE. I don't want to fight

FUNMI. Oh it is NOT enough to just say that, babe

ALICE. You didn't want me to pay you!

FUNMI. I said that did I?

ALICE. You said, buy us a puppy and fuck me all day and we're good

FUNMI. IF you can't pay me cash, big old IF, / is what I said

ALICE. And I can't, I have to have a paper-trail for everyone for the audit

FUNMI. So where's the puppy Alice? Where's our puppy? Where. Is. The. Puppy?

–

Okay, audit, okay, paper-trail, okay, bank transfers only, okay that was a very hot weekend, but bitch better have my puppy

[*An optional line if the scene plays in a way where it can take the silliness:*]

A doggy's what you owe me

ALICE. –

I don't understand why you won't just let me show you how to do your fucking taxes

FUNMI. Because it is BORING

ALICE. Meaning it's your CHOICE to be weird about freelance income, YOUR choice to not declare any of it even though it makes you paro when you don't, good luck with that when your TV ad comes out, which I put you up for by the way, / so no I'm not Evil I'm just overly indulgent of your fear of form eleven, fuck me

FUNMI. It's hurtful, I find it, it hurts me that you don't take me seriously

ALICE. –

I do

FUNMI. You don't, you Like my poems but YOU are the Real Artist, and actually I'm Real too

ALICE. You think I think that?

FUNMI. Don't you?

   ALICE's *phone goes. She checks it and makes a noise.*

   Who is it?

ALICE. Anna

FUNMI. You can take it

ALICE. They can wait

   She nopes the call and puts her phone away.

   If we're, I'm hurt that you never stand up for me with Ed

FUNMI. –

   Yeah?

ALICE. I know he doesn't like me, but you let him be mean to me

FUNMI. Ed does like you

   ALICE *makes a noise.*

   No he does, he just doesn't trust you

ALICE. Fab

FUNMI. He's convinced you're going to run away unless I nail you down

ALICE. I asked you to move in with me

FUNMI. I know

ALICE. And I've said I'll marry you if you want

FUNMI. Excuse me while I swoon

ALICE. You know what I mean

FUNMI. It's actually not about you

ALICE. It feels like it's about me

FUNMI. No, it's about Ed and how Ed would run away if he was you

ALICE. Because he'd be sleeping with his sister?

FUNMI. You know he doesn't let King say I love you?

ALICE. Why not?

FUNMI. Because he can't say it back, so it stresses him out, but now he's miserable because King DOESN'T say it

ALICE. –

Poor King

FUNMI. So really it's that Ed thinks you're as fucked up as he is, meaning when you say you love me you MUST be lying

ALICE. Which I'm not

FUNMI. I know!

ALICE. Lying, or fucked up

–

I amn't

FUNMI. And just to be clear, I never asked you to marry me

ALICE. I know

FUNMI. Even though it would make a lot of things a lot simpler

ALICE. But you're already here long enough, you've your stamp, all that

FUNMI. Because they listen when I tell them, do they?

NANCY re-enters holding an Insomnia coffee or equivalent, then holds the door for EDWARD close behind her.

EDWARD. Jill needs a bathroom, it's cool if she comes in right?

ALICE. Just her?

EDWARD. / No,

JILL (*simultaneous with* EDWARD*'s line from off*). No really, yizzir brilliant, I've been crying all morning over it haven't I Richie? / People standing up for each other, it's a beautiful thing

JILL and RICHIE enter. RICHIE is carrying a birdcage suitable for two parakeets/lovebirds/small parrots. Throughout all of the following, JILL needs to go to the toilet really badly but is enjoying talking at everyone too much to actually go

RICHIE. / Floods /

JILL. and I just so feel so lucky yer man was passing by and saw, got everyone down, can't thank yiz enough, / because it's scary enough even with everyone there, the whole thing

EDWARD. / It's what we're for! /

JILL. No knock, there's people in your bedroom looking down at you in the bed all of a sudden, and hiya Funmi! / And hiya Alice!

FUNMI. / Hi Jill /

ALICE. / Hi! /

JILL. Should have said right off, thanks for letting us in to your show, brill stuff is starting back up isn't it? But they're in your bedroom, a drill starts going somewhere, yer man the locksmith at the front door, they're grabbing your stuff, fucking it about, and they carried you out the house, didn't they Richie?

RICHIE. Fucking pricks

JILL. No shoes on even, had you Richie?

RICHIE. Still in bed when we heard them at the door, lucky I had jocks on

JILL. And they were animal about it, big fella had you off your feet by your neck for a bit / didn't he Richie?

ALICE. / Fuck /

FUNMI. / Oh my god /

NANCY. / Christ /

RICHIE. Whatever about him, I want to know who the fucking prick was let Brandon and Bruce out

ACT TWO 201

JILL. Stop or I'll be off again [crying] – (*To* ALICE/FUNMI.) you haven't seen them?

ALICE. Who?

RICHIE. The cockatiels, one of the security lads opened the cage to keep us busy, and that's on Damien's say-so I'd fucking bet

JILL. Stop, / he's demented over them

FUNMI. / Damien's your landlord? /

RICHIE. / Yeah /

JILL. And okay we're not supposed to have pets, but I said to him, we're supposed to have a microwave Damien, didn't I Richie?

RICHIE. And four rings

JILL. AND a four-ring cooker not just a hotplate, so if it's technicalities, plus we got no notice did we Richie?

RICHIE. Fucking, bedroom door banging open was the notice

JILL. And they're birds, like, they're not chewing on the furniture are they Richie?

RICHIE. Well

JILL. No I know but they're not puppies, are they? Like they'd go for your keyboard keys and wires, but that's all our stuff, and they don't get into the press and eat a thing of Cheerios and have the squits all over the floor, do they Richie?

ALICE. And that's why?

RICHIE. We're booted?

ALICE. Or is the excuse, even

RICHIE. Nah, he's a racist cunt is why, we're behind like everyone's behind because, you know, COVID, no one's working, but he owns three of them over the way from us, I know Jamie hasn't paid fucking, you know, an pingin rua in six months, he's on his own AND he's a musician, what's he been doing for lockdown? Why's he not gone?

JILL. Said that to him when he turned up, didn't you Richie?

RICHIE. Go to the toilet Jill

JILL. Oh yeah, is it – [here? nearby?]

ALICE. Through there, the door doesn't lock

JILL. You're a star, Alice

JILL exits.

RICHIE. Cheers Alice, alright Nancy?

NANCY. Sorry about all this, Richie

RICHIE. I mean, look

ALICE. You two know each other?

RICHIE. From poetry stuff, yeah, I'm a big Nancy fan

NANCY. Stop

RICHIE (*quoting/in-joking*). Ore of the womb in the mint of the palm!

NANCY. Oh god

ALICE. This fucking city

RICHIE. Kids are coins, bullion versus currency, nature versus nurture, love that poem

NANCY. Thanks Richie

ALICE (*to* NANCY). You're a poet!

NANCY. I've written poems

RICHIE. And you?

ALICE. What?

RICHIE (*to* NANCY). You come to show support? Slumlords out?

NANCY (*mindful of* ALICE). For Alice's show actually

RICHIE. No way – (*To* ALICE.) today is it?

EDWARD. Good question

ALICE. –

If we can get you sorted out

RICHIE. Ah look, we'll be fine

Bang from off, like a chair that someone is standing on suddenly tipping over.

KING (*from off*). MOTHERFUCKER

–

(*From off.*) I'M OKAY

KING *enters and everyone looks at him.*

It was so weird, it was like are we in Barcelona all of a sudden? But then we were saying no it's probably someone's pet, / anyway there was a parakeet on the roof

RICHIE. Ours, one of our two, and they're cockatiels

KING. Okay! Cool, I tried to get, him? [gender of bird?] / to hop onto my hand but then the chair turned over

RICHIE. / Is he still there? And was there just one? /

KING. And I think the noise startled him so he flew across the road but you can still see him, / just one that I saw yeah

RICHIE (*shouting to* JILL *in the bathroom*). JILL, ONE OF THE BOYS IS ON THE ROOF, WE'RE GOING OUT NOW TO GET HIM AND SEE CAN WE SEE THE OTHER ONE

JILL (*from off*). BRILL RICHIE

RICHIE *carries everyone out the door with him in his urgency.* CIARA *re-enters from the back and goes through in the direction of the bathroom. There's a whoop of surprise from* JILL. CIARA *re-enters.*

CIARA. Sorry!

A moment. A flush, JILL *re-enters with wet hands.* CIARA *goes into the bathroom.*

THOMAS *enters from the back and sees* JILL. *A moment where they are wary of one another.*

JILL. –

   Hiya Tom

THOMAS. Hope you washed your hands

   She shows him.

   Where'd everyone go?

JILL. Hunting cockatiels

THOMAS. –

   Yeah?

JILL. Me and Richie's pets

THOMAS. Right

JILL. Brandon and Bruce

THOMAS. Like, Bruce Lee and Brandon Lee?

JILL. Exactly, because they come in pairs, die on their own, mate for life and all that

THOMAS. Bruce and Brandon were father and son though?

JILL. –

   Oh yeah, that's a bit – [not on? weird? icky?]

THOMAS. But you stuck around here?

JILL. Promise I'm not stalking you!

THOMAS. Turning up at my workplace, doesn't look good

JILL. Well you know we live just across the way?

THOMAS. King said

JILL. So maybe you took the job to be near me, you creep

THOMAS. This fucking city!

JILL. Yeah

   –

   And you know it's us that's – [being evicted? in trouble?]

THOMAS. King said, and I'm sorry

—

And maybe this is a bad time, but congratulations

JILL. What for?

THOMAS. Jane was on the bus up to Beaumont the other week, hope your nanny's doing okay by the way, but she was saying to someone on the phone she's going to be an auntie

JILL. –

This fucking city

THOMAS. Right?

JILL. And only just ten weeks, ten weeks yesterday, and the stupid cow is telling everyone

THOMAS. You didn't see that one coming, no?

JILL. No, I did, I was just sick of never saying

THOMAS. I know

JILL. So when it goes wrong you've no one to talk to

THOMAS. I know

JILL. But Jane should know better, this fucking city

—

Why were you on the 27B?

THOMAS. A date, actually

JILL. Yeah?

THOMAS. Going really good

JILL. Amazing

THOMAS. Pretty big culture gap, mind, but we're working through it

JILL. She's – [from Dublin? She's Jewish?]

THOMAS. Yeah?

JILL. What were you going to say?

THOMAS. That she doesn't like musicals

JILL. Oh

THOMAS. Or Spider-Man

JILL. Bitch

THOMAS. And she supports Chelsea

JILL. What!

THOMAS. I know!

JILL. And you always swore

THOMAS. Sorta like you with kids

JILL. –

Things change

THOMAS. It's just, I'm a great dad

JILL. You are

THOMAS. And you know that I'm, I never miss school pick-up, dinner's on the table at seven, never even late with the rent or support or anything

JILL. Yeah

THOMAS. And Richie's a poet, so what happened to Wanting Stability

JILL. Tom

THOMAS. What, I'm not allowed ask? Four years together I'm not allowed even ask?

JILL. Did I say that?

THOMAS. We break up because I'm an artist, you get with another artist and have his baby

JILL. Yeah, but he's, you know

THOMAS. What?

JILL. Good at it

THOMAS. Right

JILL. Or, I don't mean that, I mean he's doing well

THOMAS. And I'm poor

JILL. Did I say that?

THOMAS. –

And he's Black

JILL. Don't do that

THOMAS. No? Not a factor even a little bit?

JILL. Sounds like you've decided already

THOMAS. Because it'd be classic, is all

JILL. You know what's classic?

THOMAS. What?

JILL. This right here

CIARA *comes out of the bathroom.*

THOMAS. What right here?

JILL. LEAVE IT, Tom

CIARA. Should I go?

JILL. No, stay

CIARA. –

Did you see the parakeet on the roof?

JILL. He's a cockatiel, actually, / and he's ours

THOMAS. / What right here is classic? /

JILL. Me and my boyfriend's, / you're working on the show?

THOMAS. / Jill? /

CIARA. I'm the sign language interpreter

JILL. Oh deadly! Think they've gone to help Richie with the boys, / the cockatiels I mean, shouldn't be too long

THOMAS. / Don't ignore me, Jill /

CIARA. Okay! And I've realised I don't know the difference between a cockatiel and a parakeet

JILL. All parakeets are parrots but not all parrots are parakeets, / and cockatiels used to be parakeets but now they're their own family because they're more closely related to cockatoos but smaller than cockatoos

THOMAS. Tell me what you meant, this right here, me wanting to understand you? You not answering and then acting like it's my fault when I don't?

JILL (*to* CIARA). I'm so sorry about this – (*To* THOMAS.) you not taking NO for an answer is what I meant

THOMAS. –

That's a fucked-up thing to say

JILL. Not true?

THOMAS. No it's not true

JILL. Then prove it, leave me alone

JILL exits. THOMAS *moves to follow.*

CIARA. Should you?

While THOMAS *briefly considers,* ANNA *enters hot and out of breath from a cycle, and upset.* THOMAS *exits past her to go after* JILL.

You okay?

ANNA. Did you bring my lunch here?

CIARA. Because you forgot it, yeah, but I didn't get a chance – [to give it to you earlier]

ANNA. Because I've just spent ten minutes at home going through the fridge going, what the fuck, am I losing it, did I imagine cooking yesterday, why is not here

CIARA. I was trying to be nice, I'm sorry

ANNA. It was nice, thank you

CIARA. You okay?

ANNA. Went home to print the script for you, Alice never emailed it to me

CIARA. Sweetheart

ANNA. I'm sorry, I've dragged you into this fucking mess

CIARA. I've gone through it with the performers, it's really not that hard

ANNA. Yeah?

CIARA. And being real?

ANNA. Yeah?

CIARA. Lower stakes than telling a Deaf person they have AIDS

ANNA. So we're okay?

CIARA. C'mere

CIARA gives ANNA a squeeze, which is cut short as NANCY, ALICE, KING, THOMAS and FUNMI pile back in, frustrated in their search for Brandon/Bruce, to continue with show preparations. ALICE may catch the tail end of the squeeze, but not enough to be sure of what she saw just yet.

(*To the new arrivals.*) No luck?

NANCY. We haven't lost lost Bruce but he's a few streets over now, my pal Harry / used to keep parrots and when they got out –

ALICE. If this is an I Was An Edgy London Squatter Story, can it wait? (*To her cast.*) And can we be ready in five?

She turns to CIARA and blanks on her name.

CIARA. Ciara

ALICE. Sorry, did you get sorted?

CIARA. Yes, even though you didn't email Anna the script

ALICE. Okay, is sorry what you want to hear?

CIARA. Why are you asking me?

ALICE. Fine – (*To* ANNA.) sorry – (*To* CIARA.) so are you good to go?

CIARA. I've a few questions

ALICE. Go for it

CIARA. So I'm fingerspelling Pende P-E-N-D-E, King said that that's, is that right?

ALICE. Yeah

CIARA. So

Demonstrates signing and speaking what she's signing.

This piece is called *Pende*, the name of both a people and its language.

It imagines a world where art is community and community is art and neither is a product.

The Pende people make beautiful art, then hide it for years.

ALICE. Brilliant

CIARA. But I could give a sign name for Pende at the start which would be a bit, it's more visual, more immediate than spelling it every time

ALICE. That sounds great

CIARA. So if you can tell me, I had a google already but didn't get anything on what the Pende people look like or dress like today

ALICE. Cool

–

Now?

CIARA. If you can?

ALICE. –

My head's totally fucked, actually, so I can't, I might need, I've a research doc I emailed myself a while back

ALICE *goes on her phone.*

KING. If it helps, Alice, I'm more than happy to wear a bone in my nose

THOMAS (*possibly not joking*). And I know all of *Graceland* off by heart

ALICE (*without looking up*). Can we shut up please? (*To* KING.) / And that's Indigenous Australians anyway

CIARA. And tell you what, while you're in your emails

ALICE. Yeah?

CIARA. We can talk about my last question, which is payment

ALICE. Is that not sorted?

CIARA. You tell me, I've already emailed you an invoice, so why don't you pull it up and let me know if you're going to pay me or if I'm going home in the next ten minutes

CIARA *shoots* ANNA *a look.* ANNA *fingerspells C-U-N-T to* CIARA. CIARA *signs BIG cunt to* ANNA. ALICE *looks up briefly in time to catch a tiny bit of this, which adds to her suspicion that she's missing something.*

Oh, and before I forget

CIARA *goes to her bag and gives* ANNA *their lunch and kisses them.* ALICE *full-on catches this.*

ALICE. Sorry, she's your – [girlfriend?]

ANNA. And?

ALICE. You're together?

CIARA. Yeah?

ALICE. So The Interpreter we've been arguing over has been Your Girlfriend all along?

ANNA. Why does it matter?

ALICE. Why am I paying your girlfriend to do her job?

ANNA. Why are you NOT paying yours to do hers?

FUNMI. THANK you

ALICE. Jobs for the lads I have sex with, is it?

FUNMI. ALICE

ANNA. Sorry but what is your fucking problem?

FUNMI. Okay, let's all just – [chill the fuck out? not lose it?]

ALICE. You, basically, you're my problem, I wish you weren't here

CIARA. Don't speak to them like that

ANNA (*to* CIARA). I'm okay

–

Alice, I don't need this, and you don't either, we're both stressed Ay Eff, you want this to go well, I get it, first show in a long time, I really do get it because I want this to go well too, this show, this job, because the pandemic means my residency is really shaky / PLUS Brexit means getting back to the UK is suddenly really complicated

ALICE. Your residency? Girl you're from England? You'll be fine

ANNA. I mean yeah, GIRL, I kind of am, but also I was born in Uganda, in Africa, and I grew up there, in Africa, unlike you, which is why I'm here on a 1G, which is why I have to work in this gallery for like, fully half the minimum wage if you work it out hourly? Not counting the hours where you're emailing me at midnight having clearly had a few like Why Didn't You Open Up With The Keys I Never Gave Back To You, or Why Haven't You Printed The Scripts I Never Emailed You, or when I'm cycling over to Marion's house to give the keys to the American tourists who are AirBnBing it, because at least this is a gallery, at least I'm in the arts, so if I don't piss off the owner who treats me like her personal servant I can get my stamp renewed without having to be a barista again, which is the only reason I haven't taken a shit on the floor in the middle of your condescending, poorly researched, Isn't Africa Where I've Never Been MAGICAL, and fuck, the only way this exhibition could be more by the lazy undergrad numbers is if you played 'Maniac 2000' and pulled a rope and dropped a load of cowrie shells from the ceiling at the end, fuck right off

ANNA *exits*. CIARA *follows*.

ACT TWO 213

FUNMI. –

I am going to warm up outside

THOMAS/KING. Yeah

FUNMI, THOMAS *and* KING *exit*.

NANCY. –

I really like the secret art-box piece

ALICE. *Pende*

NANCY. *Pende*

ALICE. –

Thanks, but you're not really the target demographic

NANCY. So who is?

ALICE. Not really sure any more

NANCY. Stop me if – [I've told you before]

–

It makes me feel so old saying that, and it's not even because I forget

ALICE. No?

NANCY. It's more, it's I've thought so much about how to tell you, rehearsed, even, that I lose track of which bits I've actually said and which I've just imagined saying

–

I told you about the photos?

ALICE. From when, of you when you were young?

NANCY. The two sets, me when I was still at the school and the ones from when I'd just had you

ALICE. Yes, is that what you wanted to talk about today?

NANCY. Sort of

ALICE. Okay

NANCY. Do you have the time?

ALICE. If you're worried about that, then – [why the fuck are you here?]

Go for it

NANCY. All I was saying was your piece feels like that, only it's me in there as well as out here, there's this thing I'm not allowed see and the thing is me, and the person who won't let me in doesn't want anything from me, I can't sing them a song to convince them

ALICE. Oh

NANCY. It's a bad feeling but it's a good piece

ALICE. Yeah?

NANCY. I wish we could get TUSLA down here, all of them at once, and the government, everyone, so they could feel what it feels like

ALICE. It's not about adoption

NANCY. What is it about then?

ALICE. The coloniality of museum culture

NANCY. You'd sell more tickets if you said it was about adoption

ALICE. We're not selling tickets

NANCY. But you could, it's really good

ALICE. Thanks

NANCY. –

Did you read that article I sent you?

ALICE. About the Mother and Baby Homes Report?

NANCY. That one, yeah

–

You haven't read it?

ALICE. I'm really busy

NANCY. I know

ALICE. So if that's what you want to talk to me about, maybe you should just talk to me about it

NANCY. Well they interviewed me

ALICE. Okay

NANCY. And I was saying I'm tired of repeating myself

ALICE. –

Okay

NANCY. Because, and this was in the article, I wanted to say my piece publicly about St Finbarr's twenty years ago and didn't get to, and I wanted to say my piece publicly about having you in Bessborough to this lot, but the commission was split into the investigation committee and the confidential committee, and do you even know the difference?

ALICE. No

NANCY. It was in the article

ALICE. I get it

NANCY. But fair enough I suppose, most of us didn't either, handy for them that lots of people gave testimony to the confidential crowd without realising that that's just Background, that's not Testimony, much less Evidence, nothing you say REALLY counts unless you say it to the investigation committee we didn't tell you about, and do you know how many people got to do that?

ALICE. No

NANCY. It was in the article

ALICE. Okay

NANCY. Less than one hundred, not including me, less than one hundred faciling of all them with all of their where's your evidence of us hiding evidence, if we didn't write it down we can't have done it, so in the end, and this is in the article, I talk to the confidential committee, not to prosecute but just to go on the record, to help Bear Witness, I go to Baggott Street and I say what I have to say and I wait and I wait and then the reports come out and it's, it's, it's, did you even read it?

ALICE. Enough to know it's insulting

NANCY. No direct quotes, you're reading three thousand pages looking for your own words or what they've made of them, how are you even supposed to know, but some of it you manage to recognise, Roseanna, she died before the report came out so she didn't get to see that they printed something like her testimony, about coming back from that foster family in tatters, split bleeding bruises on the soles of her feet, couldn't brush her hair for the sores, pregnant at fourteen, begging not to be sent back to them, what do they do only send her back, and where did they print their version, their summary, of all that?

ALICE. I don't know

NANCY. Right before the paragraph about people whose foster parents were Only Lovely, the lucky ducks, oh well, swings and roundabouts, you win some you lose some. Hugh, arrives to his foster parents and he's solid keloid from his nipples to his navel, that's not in there. No Evidence, probably, especially not now since he died the other week, pneumonia not COVID, but he died because he wouldn't go to hospital. Small wonder. And maybe he's lucky that he never had to read the fucking thing. And now they're telling us the confidential committee destroyed the tapes, didn't make transcripts, their words about our words are all that's left of all that heartache after years and years and years, and I wouldn't be surprised if they're lying through their fucking teeth about destroying it but even if they're not it might nearly be a mercy, because some of us GDPRed the records they did have of us, and this was in the article, but do you know what we got back?

ALICE. No

NANCY. A few sides of paper with boxes to tick, a literal box-ticking exercise, tick rape, tick baby died, tick incest, tick trouble sleeping, I talked for hours and mine just says I've had Gender And Sexual Identity Problems, which is almost funny because my ex always wanted me to be More Obvious

ALICE. –

I'm sorry

NANCY. So I'm thinking of going on hunger strike

ALICE. –

What?

NANCY. Because it worked for Tom Sweeney back in the two thousands with the Industrial Schools stuff, Redress Board say take the money and shut up, he says no I want my hearing so I can say my piece, they say okay but cut the offer by half, he says fuck that and goes on hunger strike, he gets the full amount they offered him in the first place, and I want that, or, I need that, because this isn't a threat, I don't want to die, but if this is what it's going to be for another five, another ten fifteen twenty years, We're Looking Into It, Any Day Now, Fuck Off And Don't Speak Unless Spoken To Like A Good Girl, Are You Sure That Happened, But Are You REALLY Sure, Was It Definitely Bleach They Put In Your Mouth, Oops You Died We're Off The Hook, / Sorry But Not Really

ALICE. Stop, please, I understand

NANCY. It's enough to make anyone, to drive you to, but we're strong. They've no idea how strong we are because they've no idea what we've lived because they just won't listen, and they'd love it if we all just died and the problem went away, but I eat porridge in the mornings now

ALICE. What?

NANCY. Never ate breakfast, not unless coffee and a cigarette counts, but I do now, porridge every morning and a fizzy vitamin, C and all the lads and calcium for my bones, iron of course, I've started waiting for the green man and I still look both ways when I cross because I don't take risks any more. I'm not going anywhere. I'll live to a hundred just to spite them. I don't take risks any more unless it's for a really good fucking reason, and this, all this is, this is it for me

ALICE. This is what you'd risk dying for

NANCY. Yes

ALICE. On hunger strike

NANCY. Yes

ALICE. –

Do you want me to say don't?

NANCY. What?

ALICE. I understand, you're furious, you're, but you say it yourself that if you die the problem goes away, so is this really a protest or is this about getting my attention?

NANCY. –

You know, when I saw that article about you and it said that you were an artist, that you had submitted an entry for the residential care memorial, that was what did it more than your age or your look? You were picking fights that weren't yours to pick. That made me want to be related to you, and then what do you know, we are, thirty-odd years you'd just been down the road. And you said you didn't want another mother, fair enough, I respect that, I didn't want a daughter, what I wanted was, I came here today looking for support. Solidarity even. But maybe you're not very good at that any more?

ALICE. If I ever was

NANCY. I know I disappointed you

ALICE. What?

NANCY. That I wasn't, that meeting me wasn't what you'd hoped for

ALICE. No

NANCY. No?

ALICE. No, it's – [not that? more complicated?]

You know that I don't talk to my adopted family because they're not very nice people

NANCY. You said

ALICE. And so I had built it all up in my head, that somewhere out there there was an Alice who was, this is mortifying

NANCY. Go on

ALICE. That somewhere out there there was an Alice who was a Hashtag Proud Hashtag African Hashtag Queen because she wasn't adopted

NANCY. And you're not that?

ALICE. No, really no, because, you turn up and you tell me my dad was like me

NANCY. Like you how?

ALICE. Irish, not from Africa, mixed or Black or whatever but in the way where other Black or mixed or whatever people think you're fucking weird because you don't know anything about anything, and, this is fucked up, I know it is, but it feels really unfair that other adopted people have this Shadow Self who they could have been Were Things Otherwise but no, I was just always going to be intense and offputting and gay

NANCY. –

Sorry?

ALICE. I do want to know you

NANCY. Yeah?

ALICE. You've a lot to say and most of it is interesting

NANCY. If you DARE call me a Queer Elder now, I will slap you

ALICE. Wouldn't dream of it

NANCY. –

I wondered if you'd join me, maybe

ALICE. –

On hunger strike?

NANCY. Not as, not like a Mother-and-Daughter thing, Jesus

ALICE. Okay

NANCY. But as, both born in homes, you were adopted and I wasn't, we're the two sides of that coin anyway

ALICE. We are

NANCY. And I know you've lots of, that all this [*your* life] is urgent, but not everything that's important is urgent. So sometimes you have to make it urgent.

Raised voices, off. There is a moment when diffuse anger becomes focused outrage. There isn't a concerted chant, but if there's a slogan it's 'SLUMLORDS OUT'. FUNMI *re-enters holding her nose, which is bleeding, followed closely by* EDWARD, THOMAS, JILL, RICHIE *(still holding the birdcage)*, CIARA, ANNA, KING.

JILL *(from off)*. Feel good about yourself, do you? This what you wanted to happen?

THOMAS. At least I did something

KING. Tilt it back

EDWARD. Don't tilt it back, that makes you choke

ALICE *(to* FUNMI*)*. Are you okay? / Jesus Fucking Christ what happened?

FUNMI. / I'm fine, honestly /

JILL. Some of the goons 'accidentally' smashed our plant pots, people were getting thick with them, nothing too wild until Tom decides it's a great idea to get aggro and starts pushing one of them out the door, it all kicks off, poor Funmi gets a shove and hits the deck, and now the Gardaí have got people on the ground and over bonnets, gloves off

ALICE. The security team or – [protesters]?

EDWARD. What do you think?

FUNMI. I'm fine, it's nothing, I'm EMBARRASSED

RICHIE. I got him back for you, Funmi, clattered him with the cage

ANNA. What now?

KING. If they're arresting everyone it's kind of game over, isn't it?

EDWARD. They're not arresting everyone, they can't arrest everyone and they don't want to arrest everyone, they want to scare us into leaving so that they can leave too and the goons can do whatever the fuck, THAT'S game over, so now is the MOST important time to make it clear we're not going anywhere, but we also shouldn't be stupid in case they do arrest people so, icky part, getting Into It, who's on for pushing their way into the house AND can afford to maybe get arrested?

NANCY's hand goes up straight away.

ALICE. Can afford to as in – ?

EDWARD. As in, and you should know this babe, as in Is A Citizen

ALICE. Okay

EDWARD. Amongst other things

ALICE. Yeah okay

ALICE's hand goes up a moment before JILL's. KING half raises a hand.

KING. –

I am, but my little brother isn't, post-2004 and his dad's American, it's fucking, it's a whole fucking thing, and they're already killing us on the reckonable residence so –

EDWARD. You can't, that's okay, that's why we ask

THOMAS. Richie, you're not?

RICHIE. Born in the UK man

KING. Your ma's Irish though?

RICHIE. Born in the UK too cos my nanny wasn't married, so we'd need HER birth cert and guess what

NANCY. She was adopted

RICHIE. Hole in one

Focus moves to THOMAS whose hand is also not really up or down.

THOMAS. –

I actually don't know?

JILL. Your ma was so you are, Tom

THOMAS. Okay

> EDWARD *looks at* NANCY, ALICE, JILL, *and* THOMAS*'s raised hands.*

EDWARD. Four out of ten, wow, okay, / not Terrible, but –

RICHIE. Tom, yer man was saying to the Gards you assaulted him so you shouldn't go back out

THOMAS. I don't care

JILL. Don't be fucking thick, you're a da

THOMAS. Fine

EDWARD. And actually Jill, you're the tenant, I know they don't need an excuse but let's still not give them one

THOMAS. Plus you're pregnant

EDWARD. –

> (*Registering new info along with everyone else.*) Another very good reason

RICHIE. You told him?

JILL. I didn't tell him, he found out

RICHIE. Yeah?

JILL. Yeah

RICHIE. Okay then

JILL (*to* THOMAS). And that right there, that's what you could never do

> CIARA *suddenly raises her hand.*

CIARA. I would, I'd like to, but some months I get Garda vetted like six times for / six different organisations –

EDWARD. Yeah, don't then

RICHIE (*his attention caught by something outside*). FUCK

ALICE. What?

RICHIE. Think I just saw Brandon fly by

ACT TWO 223

RICHIE *exits at speed.* ANNA *raises their hand.*

ANNA. I don't, I'm not a citizen but I can

CIARA. Yeah?

EDWARD. You sure?

ANNA. I'm fucked anyway

CIARA *makes a move to comfort her.*

Don't, please, I'm, I'm not fine but I know what I want to do, and it's not living here

–

(*To* CIARA.) Sorry, but – [it's the truth? it's not about you?]

CIARA. No, I know

ANNA *abruptly exits, and* CIARA *follows.*

KING (*to* EDWARD). And come to think of it, you're talking like you're leading the charge

EDWARD. I'm the union person

KING. But you definitely can't be arrested

FUNMI. Don't be stupid Ed

KING. Ed, baby, I, I am, I King David Amoah Admire you, I Admire you so much that I just used my full name for emphasis, / which I do NOT love

EDWARD. / King /

KING. Whisht, I'm not going to embarrass you if you don't embarrass yourself, I Admire you, I Admire that you don't want to ask anyone to do anything you're not doing, but it's not a complicated job, the job is Be There in the house and don't pick any fights they haven't picked first, so please just chill out and stay here with me

–

(*Coy.*) I'm so FRIGHTENED

EDWARD. Fine

NANCY (*to* EDWARD). I'm under strict instructions not to tell any more stories from my London years, but I know the rules

EDWARD. Okay then

NANCY (*to* ALICE). Me and you kid

ALICE. Yeah

NANCY. Okay?

ALICE. –

Okay

As the act ends, the sealed space of Alice's art piece Pende *explodes – figuratively or literally, as you see fit. Inside it, there is a tiny eighties bedsit. The man we've been thinking of as* RICHIE *is nude in the bed, and the woman we've been thinking of as* CIARA *is under the covers from the waist down with a bra on. Maybe a T-shirt too, and not just for the cold. For a loaded moment we look at them looking at each other. Blackout.*

ACT THREE

The ENSEMBLE *deliver bolded text, in whatever allocation you find most suitable/convenient/resonant.*

The beginning, not for the first time, is after

Because too much has already happened to tell

Recently she wasn't, but she is wearing her bra again

Recently it wasn't, but his breathing is quiet again

His flesh against hers is warm, and it leaves a brief mark when it moves

Whiter on the already white, and then the blood rushes back

The scars, always paler than pale, stay so

Where his mouth was the cold air stings

And all of this is all at once unbearable

WOMAN *dislodges* MAN's *embrace. She makes a great production of finding her knickers near the bed and putting them on without coming out from underneath the covers.* MAN *watches, bemused/amused.*

MAN. You cold?

WOMAN. No?

MAN. Alright

WOMAN. Are you?

MAN. No!

WOMAN. Because I can turn on the – [space heater]

MAN. You're getting dressed, I meant

WOMAN *tries to reach the space heater from the bed, but can't quite. She finds her top and puts it on with the same level of discretion she used when she was putting on her knickers. Only once she's got it on does she get up, go to the space heater, turn it on.*

I'm fine, don't be doing that for me

WOMAN. Well, most nights it only gets colder

MAN. Alright

WOMAN. Better to turn it on before we need it

WOMAN *sits back down on the bed but doesn't lie down. He reaches out for her but she doesn't lean into the touch.*

MAN. –

You feeling shy?

WOMAN. No?

MAN. Good

WOMAN. And why's that?

MAN. Because you're gorgeous

Once he's said this, there's a future where she says

WOMAN. YOU'RE gorgeous

And once she's said that, there's a future where they stay in bed all the next day

Steal a bottle of milk from the doorstep of one of the actual terraced houses where actual families live in actual Rathmines

Drink it all between them, rather than go the minute further past the actual terraced house to the actual shop for actual food

Decide to move to Thatcher's England together because fuck it, it can't be worse

Realise it can be worse because Ireland may hate unmarried couples but at least skinheads don't dance on unmarried couples

> **Rent a horrible little flat with no curtains above a pub**
>
> **So damp that clothes left on the floor grow mould**
>
> **Work at making it theirs, bamboo blinds the racist auld one next door despises, a mandala on the wall with the worst of the water stains**
>
> **So that by the time they realise they're having a baby it's easy for him to say**

MAN. Why not?

WOMAN. Yeah?

MAN. We're not rich but that's not what they need is it? Fancy stuff? Caviar and Champagne?

WOMAN. If you put it like that

MAN. I mean, love's the thing, isn't it?

> **And once he's said that there's a future where she says**

WOMAN. I suppose it is, yeah

> **And once she's said that there's a future where they get married for the sake of the kid who never comes home from the hospital, oops**
>
> **Or they get married and the kid grows up with an English accent, and sometimes she tries to tell herself that's why her all-in-all nice life makes her so sad**
>
> **Or once he's said**

MAN. I mean, love's the thing, isn't it?

> **There's a future where she says**

WOMAN. The other week I had Sharon with the short hair from next door around for tea and we ended up going to bed at three in the afternoon after she kissed me, and I sort of knew she would, which is sort of why I asked, so yes love IS the thing but I don't know that that means we should have a baby

And once she's said that, there's a future where he says

MAN. But we're together

WOMAN. We are

MAN. And I'm good to you, amn't I?

WOMAN. You are, you're so good to me, but – [all the same]

MAN. Go on

WOMAN. Never mind

MAN. Well you've started now

WOMAN. But none of this feels good, it was just easier

MAN. Than what?

WOMAN. Whatever else was in front of me

MAN. –

First time I'm hearing about it

WOMAN. First time I've known

MAN. Known what?

WOMAN. That I was, or that things could be, that I could do something else

And there's a future where she doesn't say that because he didn't say

MAN. I mean, love's the thing isn't it?

Because she never fell pregnant by him, never fell pregnant for the first time, never did a decade of men with as little passion as she did childhood decades of the rosary, never did any of it in a world where age eleven Maggie Stanley's skirt rode up so that Maggie Stanley's bare hot June leg touched HER bare hot June leg under the school desk, which made her want to own a bike just so that Maggie Stanley could push her off it and then kiss both her bleeding knees better to say sorry

But we can't get there from here

To that future from this moment

We'd have to go back further

Before she met him for the first time

Before she fell pregnant the first time

Before she went to a school that had no classes, as such, and as such had no Maggie Stanleys to sit beside

Before she was born, even

Before her unmarried mother fell pregnant with her, maybe

Before her mother was her mother, before the country was the country, before the world was the world

It's hard to know where to stop if we don't stop here

But once he's said

MAN. You're gorgeous

There's a future where she says

WOMAN. That's an easy thing to say

And once she's said that, there's a future where he leaves not long after

And once he's left there's a future where she doesn't realise she's pregnant until it's too late to try find a number to call, too late to get to a hospital, too late to do anything but sit on the floor between the space heater and the chair and breathe through the pain

And once she's sitting on the floor there's a future where the pain eases because it's all over and she's holding a baby she doesn't know what to do with

Or where the pain eases because she passes out

And once she's passed out, there's a future where someone finds them still on the floor days later, mother and baby still one flesh that tore and bled as it failed to split

All that happens somewhere we never get to see, but here he says

MAN. You're gorgeous

And she says

WOMAN. Ah stop

MAN. Don't believe me?

WOMAN. Should I?

MAN. –

Yeah

WOMAN. –

I always think it's so funny that that's what they're called

MAN. Yeah?

WOMAN. Space heaters, that people just looked at them and said oh yeah, they're alien spaceships

MAN. Oh

WOMAN. And you have to wonder, is that just since *Close Encounters* and *Star Wars* and them or was it all along

MAN. But is it not because they Heat Spaces?

WOMAN. –

Oh

MAN. Rooms, I mean, not because they're From Space

WOMAN. That makes sense

–

I had a moment there the other week

MAN. Oh yeah?

WOMAN. I have this job typing Mondays and Fridays, they're nice for estate agents but it's all very, you know

MAN. An Office

WOMAN. An Office, you have to wear your Nice Blouse and your Nice Skirt and your Nylons, end of the second day I'm always shattered and the other week I came in and just took all of it off and lay down on the bed, fell asleep, next thing I'm waking up to this SMELL

MAN (*leaping ahead*). You didn't

WOMAN. I did, I'd put the heater on and then thrown the tights over it, I wake up and they're not just melted they're sizzling

MAN. Ah jaysus

WOMAN. But I'm still half asleep, so what do I do only grab them

MAN. You silly goose

WOMAN. And I don't know if you've ever – [done that? burned plastic?]

MAN. Stuck to your hand?

WOMAN. Stuck to my hand isn't the half of it, I grab them and they stick to me and I'm trying to shake them off but that's just making little drops go everywhere, and I'd taken everything off remember

MAN. Ah jaysus

WOMAN. So I've got these little burns from all these little bits of plastic all over me, I go to the sink to splash some water on them, that makes them go solid, guess what she does then

MAN. What did you do?

WOMAN. Pulled them off

MAN. And that's bad?

WOMAN. If the burn is deep enough that the skin comes off with them it is, yeah

MAN. Oh no! You poor poppet

WOMAN. So that's what all the scars are if you noticed them, the fruit of my wisdom

MAN. I didn't

WOMAN. Plámás

MAN. I didn't! Where?

WOMAN. Like I'm going to point them out?

MAN. After telling me the story? Or are you spoofing?

WOMAN. How dare you

MAN. I'm a straight-shooter, you spoof me I'll call you a spoofer

WOMAN. Steady on now

MAN. Steady on yourself, spoofer

WOMAN. Here –

She shows him by lifting her top very slightly. He holds it in place, and after a moment she takes her hand away and lets him.

MAN. –

Oh yeah

–

That's nothing, that'll heal up just fine

WOMAN. Lighting candles

MAN. If you're worried, you should rub some shea butter on them

WOMAN. Oh yeah?

MAN. It's magic

WOMAN. Bit of a queen, are we? Die sooner than have a wrinkle?

MAN. You calling me a poof?

WOMAN. No

MAN. Because I'm not a fucking queer

WOMAN. Right then

MAN. Skin like mine you have to take care of it, is all, doesn't mean you take it up the arse

WOMAN. Didn't know that

He moves her top to display more of her skin. She wants to stop him but doesn't.

MAN. You alright?

WOMAN. –

Yeah

MAN. Nothing I haven't seen already

WOMAN. –

Yeah

He is sensitive to her wariness but continues. He is slow and cautious as he looks.

MAN. And is that one?

WOMAN. Yeah

MAN. And is that one?

WOMAN. That's a stretchmark

MAN. –

Oh yeah?

WOMAN. Never heard of those, skinnymalink?

MAN. I've loads, and says you, skinnymalink melodeon legs

WOMAN (*piqued by this bizarre turn of phrase*). WHAT?

MAN. What what?

WOMAN. Skinnymalink what?

MAN. Skinnymalink melodeon legs, do you not know that one?

WOMAN. You're winding me up

MAN. I'm not! It's, I don't know if it's a skipping rhyme or, but it's one of those things kids say

WOMAN. So how does it go then

MAN. Skinnymalink melodeon legs, umbrella feet
Went to the pictures but couldn't get a seat

When the picture started, skinnymalink farted
Skinnymalink melodeon legs, umbrella feet

WOMAN. Why's he got melodeon legs and umbrella feet?

MAN. I don't know, what's a malink?

WOMAN. I never heard that in my life

MAN. You must have

WOMAN. –

Must be a Dublin thing

MAN. Maybe

WOMAN. And I don't see any stretchmarks

MAN. Around here – (*Armpits.*) especially since I started lifting weights

WOMAN. They look nice on you

MAN. They look nice on you too

WOMAN. Plámás, against your skin I meant, like a tattoo or something, it looks deliberate because your skin tone is so even otherwise

MAN. You joking me?

WOMAN. No?

MAN. Who's the plámáser now?

WOMAN. You're saying your skin isn't even even though it looks even

MAN. I wish

WOMAN. Your arse is covered in boils

MAN. You tell me

He flips over to display his arse, which is not covered in boils.

WOMAN. Give over

MAN. I've loads of scars all here cos I was real spotty through me teens, used to cut them shaving, which is why if you look – (*His jawline and neck.*)

ACT THREE 235

WOMAN. Oh yeah! But they're darker, I wasn't looking for that

MAN. Well that's what happens, and one of them on this side is full-on, what do you call it when it's shiny

WOMAN. Keloid?

MAN. That's the one, just from shaving like

WOMAN. Mad

Once she's said this, there's a future where there's a long long pause, after which he says

MAN. Do you go home to your ma and da much?

And once he's said this, there's a future where there's a long pause, after which she says

WOMAN. Not that much

And once she's said that, he says barely anything until he leaves soon enough

Or once he's said

MAN. Do you go home to your ma and da much?

There's a future where there's a long pause, after which she says

WOMAN. No

MAN. No?

WOMAN. I don't, or I, I never met them

MAN. Right

–

Me neither

WOMAN. No way

MAN. Swear to god, bounced around, some nice places, some not so nice, you know the way

WOMAN. I do

MAN. This one woman, right? The day I arrive she grabs me like this – (*By the chin.*) and yanks my mouth open to have a look at my teeth

WOMAN. Get out of town

MAN. Like I'm a fucking horse

WOMAN. That's disgusting

MAN. But what's strange is, I was bringing it up because I've no scars from any of it except from shaving dry, it's gas, sort of

WOMAN. Why dry?

MAN. No hot water

WOMAN. Right

–

But would cold water not be better, even?

MAN. Some people, sometimes you wouldn't be allowed

WOMAN. –

My hands are destroyed

MAN. Yeah?

WOMAN. From the work, chemicals and all sorts

MAN. Right

WOMAN. And I get this ache

MAN. Yeah?

WOMAN. When it's cold, right down in my bones

MAN. You cold now?

WOMAN. No

MAN. Cos say the word, I'll warm you up

–

You alright?

–

Angel?

WOMAN. You know Angel isn't my real name, don't you?

ACT THREE 237

MAN. –

Might have guessed

WOMAN. Genius

MAN. Are you going to tell me?

WOMAN. What it really is?

MAN. Or are you Keeping A Bit Of Mystery

WOMAN. Well, this is it

MAN. Yeah?

WOMAN. I don't know either

MAN. –

Giz a look at you

WOMAN. Can you not see me from there, Mr Magoo?

MAN. No, I can, but giz a bit of show is what I meant

WOMAN. –

A Show?

MAN. Ah don't be like that

WOMAN. I'm very interested to hear what I'm being like

MAN. All I meant was, I'd like it if you'd lie back down on the bed for me

WOMAN. Would you now

MAN. I would, yeah

WOMAN. –

How much?

MAN. –

Loads

Once he's said this, there's a future where she says

WOMAN. No

Because even if she isn't sure she wants to refuse, she's sure she wants to be able to refuse

And once she's said that there's a future where he says

MAN. Alright then

And once he's said that there's a future where she's angry, because having refused she has to decide what happens next, which terrifies her, because whatever it is happens next it'll be her own fault

Or once she's said

WOMAN. How much?

And he's said

MAN. Loads

There's a future where she says

WOMAN. Alright then

She lies down beside him.

because the habit of going along is so old, and doing anything else terrifies her too

He kisses her lightly. He jokingly rearranges her limbs like she's a life-drawing model, makes a fuss of how good she looks now. He kisses her deeply.

And once she's said that and he's kissed her there's a future where the kiss becomes something else, and the something else becomes something else, and with one thing and another they're here for a long time after she wanted him gone, so that when he does finally leave she decides never to call because why did he stay so long when she didn't want him to

Or once she's said that and he's kissed her there's a future where she says

WOMAN. Just a sec

MAN. Of course

And once he's said that there's a future where there's a long long pause before he says

MAN. You alright?

> **And once he's said that there's a future where she says**

WOMAN. Yeah

> **Though it's clear she means no, which is why he doesn't argue when she finds an excuse to have him leave**
>
> **Or once he's said**

MAN. Of course

> **There's a future where there's a long long pause and he continues to wait, and continues to wait, and continues to wait**

WOMAN. –

I didn't like that much

MAN. Which?

WOMAN. That joke, making out like I'm your model

MAN. I'm sorry then

WOMAN. You didn't like it when that woman grabbed your chin did you?

MAN. No, I didn't

WOMAN. So you wouldn't like it if, you've told me that and straight away I grab you, force your mouth open

MAN. No, I wouldn't

WOMAN. Well then

MAN. –

Is that the same?

WOMAN. It feels like that to me

MAN. Alright

WOMAN. Because I had someone, I used to have to pose for them, and I hated it, so – [there you go? That's why]

MAN. I'm sorry, I didn't know that

—

Do you want a cuddle or will I leave you alone?

When she doesn't answer, he lays his hand face-up on the bed. Eventually she takes it.

WOMAN. I haven't said that before

MAN. No?

WOMAN. To anyone, it sounds so – [ridiculous? implausible? fucked up?]

MAN. I'm with you

There's a future where they go to London together but without their daughter and break each other's hearts

Where she goes to London alone and works out a few things

Where she dies, still young, in London, in a car accident, having never seen those photos again

Or dies not so young in an accident having never met her daughter

Or dies not young but too soon of COVID

Or dies not young but too soon into a new stage of her relationship with her daughter when a Garda keeping the Síocháin at an eviction pushes her, she goes over, hits the deck hard enough for fractures despite all her fizzy vitamins with calcium, hard enough to bounce her brain off her skull and start the bleed that doesn't stop, despite all her iron

Or dies sooner than she should have on hunger strike with no answers

Or dies having had a good run, having won some battles but lost the war, gotten half-answers that incriminate only the dead and never too much

Or dies on the battlefield, watching a church go up in flames she lit, watching the Dáil go up in flames she lit,

watching it all go up in flames she lit and who dares to say that's too far

Where they raise their daughter together in Ireland and it works until it doesn't

There's a future where she never says

NANCY. You and me kid

To her daughter because she never had a daughter, never had sex with this man, never forgot his name was Michael because she never knew in the first place, never met him, never did any of it, never went through any of it, was never taken from her mother, in a world where no children were taken, where contraception was never not legal so maybe she never existed any more than her daughter did, or should that be didn't, but either way where no one ever had to hear their white adoptive mother call a football player that word

But we can't get there from here

To that future from this moment

We'd have to go back further

Before her mother's mother was her mother's mother, before countries were countries, before the world was the world, before anyone was wronged if that was ever even a time

It's hard to know where to stop if we don't stop here

But once he says

MAN. I'm with you

There's a future where he then says

MAN. Shush a mo

WOMAN (*lower*). What?

MAN. You hear that?

WOMAN. No?

MAN. Like a tap on the door or something

WOMAN (*normal*). If you're taking the piss – [fucking don't]

MAN. I'm not! It wouldn't be your landlord, no?

WOMAN. No

MAN. Or your neighbours wanting to join in?

WOMAN. Ugh, stop

MAN (*role-playing*). We couldn't help hearing…

WOMAN. Give over

MAN *gets up and moves to leave*

Put something on, would you?

MAN. You ashamed of me?

WOMAN. Yes

MAN *puts on a T-shirt and underwear, briefly goes offstage into the 'corridor'. We hear a door.* WOMAN *looks after him but doesn't move from her position. She listens intently. We hear the door again. He returns holding an actual swear-to-god cockatiel in his hands.*

MAN. Look who I found!

WOMAN. You're not serious

MAN. Just hanging around in the hall, poor little fella is VERY lost

WOMAN. What time is it? Who's letting their budgie out now?

MAN. I think he's a parakeet?

WOMAN. Are those not the same thing?

MAN. –

I actually don't know

WOMAN. And what'd you bring him in for?

MAN. He was flapping around like mad and I was worried he was going to hurt himself, banging off the doors and into the walls and banisters and all that

ACT THREE 243

WOMAN. Was that the noise?

MAN. That I heard?

WOMAN. Yeah

MAN. I think so, yeah, do you know do any of your neighbours have birds?

WOMAN. We're not supposed to have pets

MAN. Right, fair enough, where would they even go in a place like this (*Bedsit.*)

WOMAN. Or he could have come in from outside

MAN (*to the cockatiel*). Warmer than out there, right buddy?

WOMAN. Just about

MAN (*to the cockatiel*). And look at you now, good as gold, calmed right down when we started chatting didn't you?

WOMAN. Does he have any kind of, isn't it rings for birds?

MAN. A collar with his name on it, you mean?

WOMAN. Or just any way of knowing where he's from

MAN. Total mystery bird

–

What'll we call him?

WOMAN. Do you think we're keeping him? This is someone's pet, / they're going to miss him

MAN. No I know, but do you want to go knocking on doors now?

WOMAN. Oh yeah

MAN. And we've already decided he's a boy, so might as well give him a name for the night that's in it

WOMAN. –

Are you alright holding him?

MAN. Ah yeah, he's nice

WOMAN. Yeah?

MAN. Fluffy, and it's funny but I thought birds would be cold

WOMAN. He's warm, is he?

MAN. Little radiator, the engine's been working hard, hasn't it buddy?

If it's safe to do so, MAN *lets the cockatiel down on the bed beside them. They watch the cockatiel.*

WOMAN. –

Is it safe to go to sleep, do you think?

MAN. For us?

WOMAN. And leave him, unsupervised sounds silly, but yeah

MAN. Where's he gonna go?

WOMAN. What if he shits on us?

MAN. How you going to stop him even if you are awake? Ask him nicely?

WOMAN. I suppose

MAN. Only thing is, what if he panics again and hurts himself, flies into the heater or something

WOMAN. So we have to stay awake

MAN. We don't both have to, you can sleep for a bit

WOMAN. Guess you're staying then

MAN. –

Were you going to boot me?

WOMAN. –

Yeah

MAN. I was going to let you name him, but now – [fat chance]

WOMAN. You go ahead

MAN. –

We'll call you Phil

WOMAN. As in Collins?

–

What?

MAN. Lynott

WOMAN. Oh yeah

MAN *moves from the bed to the chair with Phil.*

MAN. You tired?

WOMAN. A bit

MAN. You go on to sleep then, we'll be fine

WOMAN. You're just going to sit there?

MAN. You nervous? Want me to go sit in the stairwell?

WOMAN. No! Just you can sit on the bed with me, if you don't think you'll fall asleep too

MAN. Yeah?

WOMAN. Yeah

MAN *moves back to the bed with Phil. After a moment,* WOMAN *reaches out and touches him – on the arm that's holding Phil? On the back of the neck? The lower back? Familiar rather than tender.*

–

Can I hold him?

Blackout.

End.

www.nickhernbooks.co.uk

@nickhernbooks